Joseph Grange

Portland, Maine

Summer 1993.

Ontology
and the
Practical Arena

Ontology
and the
Practical Arena

◆◆◆

Douglas Browning

THE PENNSYLVANIA STATE UNIVERSITY PRESS
University Park and London

Excerpts from Gilbert Harman, *The Nature of Reality*, reprinted by permission of the Oxford University Press, © 1977 Oxford University Press.

Excerpts from Everett W. Hall, *Philosophical Systems, a Categorical Analysis*, reprinted by permission of the University of Chicago Press, © 1960 University of Chicago.

Excerpts from J. L. Mackie, *Ethics: Inventing Right and Wrong*, reprinted by permission of Penguin Books. Copyright © 1977 J. L. Mackie.

Excerpt from William A. Christian, "Some Uses of Reason," in *The Relevance of Whitehead*, ed. Ivor Leclerc, reprinted by permission of Unwin Hyman, Inc., Winchester, MA, and Unwin Hyman Ltd., London, © 1961 Unwin Hyman Ltd., London.

Excerpt from Stephen C. Pepper, *World Hypotheses, A Study in Evidence*, reprinted by permission of the University of California Press, © 1942 University of California.

Excerpts from Sextus Empiricus, *Sextus Empiricus: Selections from the Major Writings on Skepticism, Man, and God*, reprinted by permission of the Hackett Publishing Company, © 1985 Hackett Publishing Company.

Excerpt from Alfred North Whitehead, *Modes of Thought*, reprinted by permission of the Cambridge University Press, © 1938 Cambridge University Press.

Excerpt from John Dewey, *John Dewey: The Later Works*, volume 12, reprinted by permission of the Southern Illinois University Press, © 1986 Southern Illinois University Press.

Excerpts from P. F. Strawson, *Skepticism and Naturalism: Some Varieties*, Columbia University Press, reprinted by permission of P. F. Strawson. Copyright © 1985 P. F. Strawson.

Excerpts from José Ortega y Gasset, *Meditations on Quixote*, reprinted by permission of W. W. Norton and Company, © 1957 W. W. Norton and Company.

Library of Congress Cataloging-in-Publication Data

Browning, Douglas.
    Ontology and the practical arena / Douglas Browning.

        p.   cm.
    Bibliography: p.
    Includes index.
    ISBN 0-271-00677-3
    1. Ontology.   I. Title.
BD311.B76   1990
111-dc20   89-8369

For Becky

Some men refuse to recognize the depth of something because they demand that the profound should manifest itself in the same way as the superficial. Not accepting the fact that there may be several kinds of clarity, they pay exclusive attention to the clarity peculiar to surfaces. They do not realize that to be hidden beneath the surface, merely appearing through it, throbbing underneath it, is essential to depth.

To ignore the fact that each thing has a character of its own and not what we wish to demand of it, is in my opinion the real capital sin, which I call a sin of the heart because it derives its nature from lack of love.

Ortega y Gasset, Meditations on Quixote

Contents

Preface

This book falls into an area of philosophy which might be called "meta-ontology." Few of us, I suspect, are likely to launch ourselves into this rarefied climate because of its intrinsic appeal; we are much more likely to find ourselves there unwillingly, having slipped into it because of a lack of purchase in our attempts to do ontology itself. Such is certainly my own story. To put it roundly, the problems of how one goes about getting properly started doing ontology and what might count as access to its special subject-matter have been persistent impediments to my more constructive inclinations. I have not only found them to get in my own way, but I have found it hard to convince myself that very many philosophers take them seriously enough. Unfortunately, on the unraveling, if not the solution, of such issues hangs the very legitimacy of the ontological enterprise. And if ontology is as central to philosophy in general as I think it is, then more is at stake than a mere personal inconvenience.

I have come to this recognition in a way that is sure to appear circuitous. My admiration for the very different metaphysical systems of Aristotle and Whitehead and for the scope and intensity of their irreconcilable visions, coupled with the more pedestrian concerns which I have carried with me for many years of finding a central place in the nature of things for agency, loss, facts, opacity, and the distinctively moral, have combined to leave me vulnerable to insecurities about the very possibility of a viable ontology. Fed by what I took to be the failures of Cassirer, Heidegger, Wittgenstein, Everett Hall, P. F. Strawson, and others to provide some way of coming to terms with these difficulties or of getting beyond them, my insecurities were only somewhat diminished by my renewed appreciation for Dewey. Beyond this point, it would appear, I have been left to my own devices.

It is a guiding conviction (for which I argue in the first chapter) throughout the following discussion that ontological questions and the concerted attempt to answer them deserve to be taken seriously on their own merits. I do not think, as some contemporary writers apparently do, that interest in such matters is at best archeological, a concern which can be accepted as legitimate only insofar as it directs its energies to the uncovering of an outmoded and immature phase of our cultural development. I cannot agree that ontological concern is something that must or even can be outgrown. Nevertheless, I do not attempt in these pages to show why anyone *should* pursue ontological inquiry or what its payoff, if any, might be. I have never understood, for example, the purported need for an ontology to shore up morality; that would be, it seems to me, to attempt to certify the reality of something which we are already convinced on other grounds that an ontology must accommodate. Moreover, I do not assume that there is a true ontological system waiting to be discovered if only we go at things in the right way. In fact, I am quite convinced that any system, ontological or otherwise, is as pure a product of human ingenuity as a work of art. In these respects I may be thought to wade with the contemporary relativists, the historicists, or the so-called "postmodernists," but whatever water I may share with them is shallow indeed. I mention these matters here because, having other fish to fry, I do not make a point of doing so in the text.

The overall shape of this work has emerged in a graduate seminar on ontological systems which I have offered on a somewhat regular basis at the University of Texas. My procedure in this course has varied over the years, but has always revolved around a close examination of the structurally diverse sorts of ontological frameworks and the methods of approach proposed by Aristotle, Leibniz, Frege, Russell, and Whitehead. Though study of these philosophers has provided a useful means for the introduction to graduate students of the major themes of the present work, I have chosen not to double its length by following that tortuous course of development here. In any event, I would like to take this opportunity to express my profound gratitude to all of my students in this course for their receptivity, criticism, and plain patience. Charles Krecz, George Harris, Natalia Moehle, Gregory Pappas, and Dwight Van de Vate deserve special thanks for carefully and critically reading through one or more drafts of this work. So also do those editors at the Penn State Press, Dennis Goldford and Ann Bates, who took the project seriously. For the encouragement and critical stubbornness of all of these persons I owe more than I can adequately express.

In order to avoid footnotes of reference, I have adopted the device of referring to items in the bibliography within parentheses in the text itself. Such references will, I trust, be self-explanatory in context.

Introduction

◆◆◆   I propose in this work, first, to consider the process of doing ontology and, second, to argue for the importance which an understanding of practical stancing has for it. Accordingly, it is divided into two parts which address these topics in turn. Let me be a bit more specific about what this involves.

Ontology, as I shall use the term, is to be understood as a specific sort of metaphysical enterprise or concern which, whether ultimately found to be viable or not, has been and continues to be carried on by certain philosophers. To label it as "metaphysical" is merely to indicate that it raises questions about "reality," but this does not take us very far. Even the most cursory consideration of the literature reveals that when philosophers talk of metaphysics and metaphysicians they are not always talking about the same sort of thing. Among the activities to which they may be found to be referring, the following three seem most prevalent. It is only the last which will concern us.

(i) The term 'metaphysics' is sometimes taken, perhaps most often among Anglo-American philosophers, to designate a mixed bag of problems which seem to belong together because, in some manner or other, each involves claims which employ, in some important way, the notions of reality, existence, necessity, possibility, or some such similar notion. A man who "does" metaphysics in this sense is one who devotes some modicum of effort to one or more of the following sorts of topics: the problems of the nature of God, man, causality, time, and substance, the problem of free will, the mind-body problem, the indeterminism/determinism controversy, and the problem of personal identity. Moreover, often the problems of other "areas" of philosophy, such as ethics, epistemology, and logic, are taken as having metaphysical aspects. Such an aspect often seems to appear whenever one or more of the aforementioned notions, namely, reality, existence, necessity, possibility, etc., intrudes into the discussion in such a way that one must make substantive claims about its proper employment in that context. Let us call this overall area of philosophical interest *metaphysics in the liberal sense*.

(ii) Sometimes, however, the term 'metaphysics' is taken to apply to that enterprise wherein one is concerned to arrive at ultimate principles, i.e., those principles which are of the most general yet applicable sort. What is said to fall under such principles is quite everything which may be found in our experience, feeling, thought, and action—in a word, anything that may appear in our lives. When metaphysical claims are characterized as the most general which can be made, as the most inclusive, or as the necessary presuppositions of human thought and experience, it is this sense of the term which is usually being invoked. The ideal, then, of this sort of enterprise is to frame a complete and coherent set of such principles or categories. When we have them, we have gone as far as we can go in scope and ultimacy. This ideal is, in fact, often conceived as the framing of a system much like a scientific theory, but of a much broader applicability and requiring perhaps for its furtherance additional methodological motions. There are many problems internal to this enterprise, and there are the external problems of whether one can intelligibly or profitably engage upon it. But one who claims to be a metaphysician in this sense claims to be doing something quite determinate. What is being provided, it is thought, is a framework in terms of which the problems of metaphysics in the liberal sense and, indeed, all problems, philosophical or otherwise, find their intelligibility if not their solution. Let us call this area of philosophical activity *universal science*.

It is worth noting regarding the project of universal science that the term 'reality' (or 'existence', 'necessity', etc.), if it appears at all in the discourse, plays one or other of two quite limited roles. One role, which may be termed "systemic," is that of providing one category among others, of anchoring one principle among others. Of course, there is (or may be thought to be) something outside the system. The system must be applicable to something other than itself, namely, whatever properly falls within its scope. This is to say that the adequacy of the system lies in its ability (or rather, our ability in using it) to properly take into account whatever might arise within our lives. And this introduces the second possible role for terms like 'reality', which may be termed "datal," for such linguistic items arise in our lives presystemically as "data" to which the system must be adequate.

(iii) But now, some philosophers do not think that the project of universal science is "metaphysical" in the right way. They wish, instead, to hit upon those categories and principles which are true of the way things are in reality. In referring to "reality" in this way, they wish to refer to something the notion of which is not itself a category or principle within the system. Thus, given a system in which, for example, the term 'reality' appears as an ultimate notion, they wish to claim that that system, as a whole and therefore including its systemic use of 'reality', is true, not in the sense of being applicable to whatever arises in our lives, but in the sense of being true of whatever is "real," "in the universe as it really is," or simply "in reality." Clearly, then, the reference made by the term 'reality' (or its like) in this way is not simply to something over which the system is to spread its cloak of adequacy. Thus, neither role of the term as it may arise in universal science is what is involved here. This new and third possible role of the term may be called "metasystemic," for it is a role involved in making a claim about the system as a whole. Now, those who do this sort of thing, who attempt to construct and defend a system about which a claim of this sort can be made—which is what some people sometimes are thinking about when they talk of metaphysics—may be said to be doing *ontology*. The project is, thus, to provide the most general picture of the way things really are.

The term 'reality' or some such cognate term, then, functions differently in each of these areas of interest. In metaphysics in the liberal sense, it serves as a flag of commonality, as a clue that one is dealing with a problem akin to that of a somewhat different focus. Without appeal to universal science or ontology, there is nothing more to say about it. For to go so far as to say that such a term is the same in several contexts is already to move towards invoking it as in some sense ultimate, either as an ultimate explanatory notion or as marking out the ultimate subject-matter of concern. Systematic work in metaphysics in the liberal sense drives one towards the consideration of the viability of universal science or ontology.

In the former of these, as we have seen, the term 'reality' can be invoked only in a systemic or datal role, either as a term for a principle or category in the system or as a term the use of which in our lives is to be covered by appeal to such principles or categories.

In ontology, on the other hand, the term may appear, not only in these roles, but metasystemically as well. Indeed, it or a cognate term must appear metasystemically, i.e., in such a way that, by appeal to it, a claim can be made about the system. In such a use it poses a puzzle, namely, of how one can talk intelligibly about that which lies outside the scope of the very principles of intelligibility which serve to comprise the system. It is a dim recognition of this puzzle which, I suspect, has led many philosophers to the view that ontology is not only incapable of success, but impossible of formulation. It rests, they would say, on a deep and perhaps engrained conceptual confusion. Whether this is so or not (and it is one implication of the discussions in this book that it is not), the fact remains that some philosophers claim to be doing ontology and that, when they do so, they are logically committed to the claim that there is a use of the term 'reality' or the like which is radically distinct from the use of the term to mark an item within or falling under the system. To put it somewhat differently, the use of the term 'reality' in ontology is to designate its subject-matter, whereas in the other two disciplines it does not serve this role at all.

It is perhaps sufficient for our purposes to mark out the sort of enterprise which is ontological by reference to its goal, namely, the achievement of a single, unified system which is true of reality as a whole or in its totality. But it is important to keep in mind that it is an enterprise and, as such, it both (1) arises out of concerns which are preontological and (2) proceeds in a distinctive fashion which attempts to remain true to those initial concerns. Let me say something about each of these characteristics.

Though its aim is to rise to the rarefied atmosphere of a system, ontological interest has its roots in the heavy and plodding affairs of our day-to-day lives. Its initial motivation arises in a reflection upon and a raising of questions about assumptions and claims which structure those affairs, and it receives its significance and its sense of evidence from that base. This grounding in affairs which are, in the strict sense, preontological and, indeed, prephilosophical in concern marks the initial pole or boundary of the ontological, just as the realization of the ideal of acceptable system marks the pole of closure.

Strictly speaking, the enterprise of ontology lies between these two poles. It is true that it cannot be fully understood apart from an appreciation of what is involved at each of them, but it is equally true that it cannot be fully understood by their consideration alone. As an enterprise, it must be seen in transit, as taking its course from one pole towards the other, as a process of reflection, inquiry, construction, and hypothesis. Moreover, since its ground is only proleptically ontological and since the achievement of a finished system may lie beyond its reach, what is most concretely ontological is just the process itself.

It is the aim of Part One of this work to provide an overview of this process and to indicate in general terms what is required, reasonable, and promising in regard to its development. Since, as just indicated, an appreciation of what is involved at both of its poles is essential to this understanding, I begin with two chapters in which each of these poles is discussed in turn, though only in such detail as seems to me sufficient for proceeding responsibly to a consideration of the process of ontological investigation itself. The third chapter, then, attempts to set out the pattern, methodological concerns, and special difficulties which confront the carrying out of this investigation.

There are difficulties enough. It has never been entirely clear, even to those who feel compelled to engage in ontology, how one is to go about designating or identifying its proper subject-matter (i.e., reality), how one is to examine or survey that subject-matter, how one is to have any confidence in speculations about it, how one is to proceed in constructing a general system, or how one is to evaluate the various proposals which may be entertained along the way. In particular, one who engages in ontology cannot help but feel the need both for guides or cues to speculation and for evidence by virtue of which one may gain some modicum of confidence about the adequacy and applicability of alternative hypotheses. Some significant access to reality would appear to be necessary, yet no such access seems quite above board and innocent. This problem of access lies at the center of the methodological difficulties of ontology. Apart from its resolution, it would appear that the ontological enterprise, as distinguished from those of metaphysics in the liberal sense and universal science, must forever founder, remaining incorrigibly adrift as to its viability and, indeed, its very meaningfulness. I propose, then, to confront this issue in the closing chapter of Part One.

Part One concludes with a general argument for the desirability, if not the necessity, of identifying, among all of the various ways of viewing or attending to things in our lives, one way which may be taken, not as an exclusive access to things as they are, but as one which is to be favored in the methodological role of providing a cue for ontological construction. It is the business of Part Two to attempt to satisfy this need. What it proposes is an approach to doing ontology which provides a pivotal role in ontological speculation and construction for attending to the structure of the situation as it is revealed from practical stancing.

Part Two will begin (in chapter 5) with a general argument for the primacy among all manners of stancing of the practical and, by virtue of this, its preferred candidacy as the favored manner of access to reality. I employ the term 'practical stancing' to cover any case of one's regarding some thing or range of things as an agent and, therefore, as a segment or part of a situation in which the regarder, as an agent, stands. Such cases can be grouped together by virtue of sharing a certain manner of regard, a manner which I shall refer to with the phrase 'the practical stance'. It is, I think, much the same manner of regard which has been variously referred to as "the practical attitude," "the practical point of view," and, at least by P. F. Strawson (36), the "participant" or "involved standpoint." I will, of course, say a great deal more about this stance in subsequent chapters, especially in chapters 1, 5, and 6.

The second chapter of Part Two (chapter 6) will be concerned with the task of setting out the general structure of those situations which are disclosed through practical stancing. There are, indeed, significant problems and difficulties which attend any such attempt. The upshot of taking these difficulties seriously is that, even upon acceptance of the favored status of practical stancing and a consequent attention to its situation, one cannot expect to find its structure revealed straight out and on its face. Nonetheless, it is my purpose in this chapter not merely to confront and discuss these difficulties but, with due regard to them, to suggest a number of general traits of practical situations which, it seems to me, any more extensive proposal of overall structure must embody. What is elicited, then, is not so much a finished picture of the practical arena, as I shall call it, but a sketch of some of its essentials. Apart from attention to these matters, I will urge, the ontologist is precluded from even the possibility of achieving a cue for his speculations.

In chapter 7 I will indicate how this evidence may aid the ontologist and, in virtue of this, the extent to which this aid serves to blunt the difficulties which stand in the way of accepting ontology as a legitimate enterprise. I will also, however, argue that appeal to practical stancing as favored access and to what is disclosed within it are not yet quite enough to provide the degree of critical control which would ensure the full and unexceptionable viability, the real possibility of theoretical success, of the enterprise. In a word, there remain two conditions on a cue which even the closest attention to the practical arena cannot alone provide, namely, its articulation in a manner which is fitted for theoretical use and its expandability to comprehending scope and power. Recognition of this brings to light the importance for ontology of our specification of a pretheoretical manner of *having a world* which both incorporates the practical arena in a way which preserves its integrity and allows itself of a theoretically available articulation. I shall close by making only the barest suggestion of how this might be accomplished, for any fuller elaboration would carry us beyond the limits of this book and into another.

What is proposed in the present work, then, is not a finished defense of the viability of the ontological enterprise but, rather, an argument for its legitimacy and, consonant with that, for the promise which our proceeding along a certain path seems to offer in our ontological investigations. My only concern is to point the ontologist in the right direction, to follow along a bit to caution against straying into another path, and then, as it seems to me I should, to leave the responsibility for the longer journey to whoever has the courage or perhaps the temerity to take it on.

Part 1

Ontology

1

The Ground
of Ontological Interest

◆◆◆ 1. In his recent book *Skepticism and Naturalism: Some Varieties*, P. F. Strawson introduces "the notion of a radical difference in the standpoint from which what are in a sense identical objects or events or phenomena may be viewed" (35). He then proceeds, in a manner reminiscent of Kant, to distinguish two such "standpoints":

> Viewed from one standpoint, the standpoint that we naturally occupy as social beings, human behavior appears as the proper object of all those personal and moral reactions, judgments and attitudes to which, as social beings, we are naturally prone; or to put the same point differently, human actions and human agents appear as bearers of objective moral properties. But if anyone consistently succeeded in viewing such behavior in what I have called the "purely objective," or what might better be called the "purely naturalistic," light, then to him such reactions, judgments, and attitudes would be alien; the notion of "proper objects" of such reactions and attitudes, the notion of "objective moral properties," would for him lack significance; rather, he would *observe* the

prevalence of such reactions and attitudes in those around him, could establish correlations between types of attitude and the types of behavior which observably evoked them, and generally treat this whole range of moral and personal reaction, attitude, and judgment as yet another range of natural phenomena to be studied; to be understood, in a sense, but not in the way of understanding which involves sharing or sympathizing with. (35)

Strawson makes the following comment about this second "standpoint":

I have described it in the conditional mood, i.e. have said how it would be rather than how it is, in order to emphasize the point which I began with: our human incapacity, as being committed to participant relationships and acting under the sense of freedom, to hold such position for more than a limited period in limited connections. (35–36)

Given these contrasting "standpoints," he then considers a certain response which might arise.

At this point one may feel a strong temptation to raise, and to press, a certain question. I have spoken of two different standpoints from which human behavior may be viewed: for short, the "participant" versus the "objective," the "involved" versus the "detached." One standpoint is associated with a certain range of attitudes and reactions, the other with a different range of attitudes and reactions. Standpoints and attitudes are not only different, they are profoundly opposed. One cannot be whole-heartedly committed to both at once. It will not do to say that they are mutually exclusive; since we are rarely whole-hearted creatures. But they tend in the limit to mutual exclusion. How natural it is, then, to ask the question: "Which is the correct standpoint? Which is the standpoint from which we see things as they really are?" (36)

Later on I will indicate why this question is misconceived and why I think Strawson's own view of why it is misconceived is nonetheless unacceptable. But apart from that, I have quoted Strawson at length in order to bring out a certain picture of our everyday concerns and of how ontological interest arises in regard to them which seems to me to be as clearly correct in some respects as it is mistaken in others.

2. The following points, some of which derive directly from Strawson's remarks and some of which involve a more or less benign reformulation of his manner of speaking, seem unexceptionable.

(1) Each of the two "standpoints" identified by Strawson, however they might properly be fleshed out, are genuine. We do take or find ourselves within them in the course of our lives, though there may be others, such as the aesthetic, which arise there as well. In fact, it would seem that our being in one or another such "standpoint" pretty much exhausts our lives. At least, those times of which we might say that we were not standing in one or another of them seem episodic or, if prolonged, confusing and disorienting. "Standpoints" represent, that is, our only ways of orientation, of understanding, of getting a grip on things.

(2) Each of the two "standpoints" mentioned is to be understood as involving, not merely distinctive manners of experiencing and conceiving things, but a native range of attitudes and actions. Indeed, we might call each a "global" way of proceeding in one's life, for each represents a way of taking account of and being concerned with whatever might be found or referred to within its compass. Of course, what appears within each appears there distinctively, so that the "objects or events or phenomena," as Strawson puts it, can be taken to be "in a sense" identical across "standpoints" only by virtue of a certain referential act which itself appears distinctively in each "standpoint." There is no antecedently presented set of "things" upon which each "standpoint" may be turned indifferently, for this would involve the invocation of a privileged third "standpoint" which could be accepted within all others, including our "detached" and "involved" ones, as foundational and self-certifying. But, of course, any such third "standpoint" would be, by virtue of its own distinctive manner of regard and presentation, just another player in the game and equally questionable in regard to its offerings. And in any case, there does not seem to be any such "standpoint" to which both the "detached" and the "involved" simply acquiesce.

(3) For this reason it will not do to take "standpoints" as merely differing perspectives upon things indifferently shared among them, i.e., as views or slants upon certain things from different positions and thus as disclosing different faces which are, in spite of their differences, attributable to those things without strain or opposition. Strawson's term 'standpoint' is on this count likely to be misleading, for the picture it suggests is of a position taken from which an antecedently available terrain may be viewed. I propose therefore to avoid calling these manners of regard "standpoints," "points of view," "perspectives," or even "attitudes," for each suggests this faulty picture in one way or another. I propose, instead, using a term which does not seem, at least to me, to be as confining. I will call them stances.

(4) It goes along with this that to speak of how things appear "from" or "to" a certain stance, as Strawson is inclined to do, is also to encourage the wrong picture. It is, rather, that things appear *within* a stance such

that, within that stance as well, the stancer may take one of a certain range of views, perspectives, or attitudes upon or towards them. Such "views" as one may take are, of course, native to that stance and available within it. Once we see this, we may continue to speak loosely of how things appear from a certain stance, so long, that is, as we understand that such things appear *from within* it.

There are two general points to be made about the language we use in discussing stances. First, in attempting to characterize stances in general, we must avoid any use of terms which is special to one particular stance, for if we don't, we run the risk (if not the certainty) of attributing to all stances what is appropriate only to the one we have chosen. Positively put, the point is that we must attempt to frame a cross-stance vocabulary. Unfortunately, this is not easily done or ever likely to be fully satisfactory with respect to the desiderata of clarity and precision of application. We have been forced in our discussion above (as has Strawson) to employ such intuitively meaningful terms as 'things', 'ways', 'appears', and 'appears as', rather than (as Strawson also sometimes does) terms which derive from and have their clearest applicability in a "detached" and theoretically purified stance, e.g., terms such as 'property', 'object', 'bearer of properties', and 'reactive attitude'. I will say something more about some of these tainted terms a bit later. Second, in indicating what is distinctive about any particular stance, we cannot allow ourselves to rely on the language of another stance, for mischaracterization or, worse, a characterization which construes that other stance as essentially confused or in error about things will surely result. In view of this, it may strike one initially as only fair to allow each stance to speak for itself and in its own idiom. But there is a limit to how much help we can get in this way, for it does not apear that every stance—and certainly not the "involved" one—is in the business of describing itself or pointing out how it is to be distinguished from other stances which may be considered to be on a par with it. Now, the overcoming of this shortfall, as well as the satisfaction of the need for a cross-stance terminology, would appear to be possible only on the condition of our being enabled to survey all stances from a position of reflective neutrality. And this seems quite mysterious, since if such neutrality represented a stance, it would be itself a player in the game, and if it represented not a stance but a perspective, it would be a captive of some specific stance and thereby also fail in neutrality. Nonetheless, we do (and Strawson certainly does) compare stances and recognize their opposition, so something must be askew about the dilemma posed. This tough issue I leave for a later discussion in this chapter. The point to be made here is just that we cannot in good conscience attempt to compare the two stances discussed or even identify them as distinct, except on the basis of what we must take to be a manner of reflection which repudiates allegiance to either.

(5) Now, as already indicated, within each stance each thing which is present or comes to be attended to appears distinctively, i.e., as being of some character which we find to be, upon comparison with other stances, unique to it. I will adopt, in accordance with Strawson's own language, the term 'appears' to indicate any manner of any presence of anything within a stance. The substantive point here is then that how something appears is in some respect always stance-bound or, to use another locution which Strawson also introduces, whatever appears within a stance always *appears as* being of a sort or character which is alien to other stances. I shall come back to the issue of what this distinctiveness comes to in a moment, for that introduces another point. But the point here may be made by contrasting this distinctiveness of how things appear which holds between stances with the sort of difference among the appearances of things which may be found within one stance. One sort of intra-stance difference in how something appears may, as we have seen, be understood in terms of perspectives. In any case, given something which we take within a stance to be one thing, the differences in how it appears in different perspectives, at different times, under differing circumstances, and so on, may serve to raise the question of what it is *really* like as opposed to what it is only *apparently* like. Questions of this sort, as well as those regarding what is genuine as opposed to spurious, trustworthy as an appearance as opposed to untrustworthy, and even veridical as opposed to nonveridical, arise naturally within a stance and have in such cases an intra-stance application only. But the question which Strawson poses is clearly not of this sort and, however much it may be taken by him to be misconceived, it is nonetheless taken by him to address a difference which is not intra-stance in scope but lies between stances and how things appear within them. That he takes this radical difference to be the case is clear from the fact that he finds the two stances he discusses to be "profoundly opposed." And it would seem that he is quite right about this.

(6) The basis for this "profound opposition" between stances does not rest on the bare fact that things appear distinctively in each stance; it can only rest on the fact that such differing characterizations are mutually excluding. This is not to say, as Strawson is at pains to point out, that one cannot slip from stance to stance or that one cannot be half-heartedly involved in more than one stance at a time, though there is a lot more to be said on half-heartedness and its possibility. It is to say that within one stance which is whole-heartedly taken or, more precisely, which is considered as such and in regard to what it would be in its purity, things ap-

pear to be such that, were they to be as they appear, they could not also be as they appear from another stance considered as such. This opposition, that is, lies in a difference among the very assumptions or conceptions regarding things which is involved in their appearing as they do in different stances, so that even from a third stance no manner of construing things could be coherently framed which bodily included both sorts of characters or features in those things. Something about how things appear to be in different stances makes them irreconcilable. Strawson brings this out in his consideration of what he refers to as "objective moral properties" as they present themselves in the "involved" stance. We need not assume, as he seems to do, that this stance and the moral stance are pretty much the same, just as we need not assume with him that this stance is somehow essentially a "social" stance. But his point in bringing up "moral properties" seems to be this. Things as they appear from the one stance can have them, but things as they appear from the other stance cannot. Whatever things are taken to be like within the "detached" stance, however they in general may appear, they cannot themselves take on "moral properties," though such purported properties (as arise within the "involved" stance and appear straightforwardly as being of certain things) may be considered and our receptivity to them (within the "involved" stance) provided with an "explanation" on the basis of processes or events (psychological perhaps) which are acceptable (within the "detached" stance).

As we have thus far discussed it, the picture which Strawson appears to present regarding stances seems, apart from some of his unfortunate language, quite persuasive. But more might be said about stances than Strawson provides, and it seems to me that in some respects what he does say suggests a mistaken reading of what this picture is supposed to represent. In the next three sections I will proceed upon this expansion and criticism.

3. We may begin by considering a bit more precisely how it can be that, though each stance is exclusive in the way indicated under point (6) above, it can nonetheless encompass the things of another stance. A stance S, we may say, can encompass something m in another stance S^* by reference and even by a certain indirect sort of description, but it is excluded from encompassing it as it appears in S^*, in its S^*-appearing form. To employ a somewhat artificial language, we may say that (i) whenever something m appears within S^* as x-being-F, m also appears within S^* as being-the-case-of-x-being-F, (ii) m cannot appear in S as being-the-case-of-x-being-F, but (iii) a reference to m can appear within S

under the designation of "*x*-being-*F*" or, more precisely, as having-ap-peared-as-being-the-case-of-*x*-being-*F*.[1]

The point of this contrived way of putting (iii) is not at all to deny that an "appearance" which arises within *S** may be remembered, imaged, or otherwise referred to within *S* and, in that way, may be said to "reappear" within *S*. The point is to allow that. But the point of (ii) is to deny that this "reappearance" can be full-bodied; something is necessarily lost, something like a "claim," "force," or "peremptoriness" which the "ap-pearance" in its first-order presence carries with it and on its face.[2] So, for example, within Strawson's "detached standpoint" the way things make their appearance within the "involved" standpoint may well be con-sidered, taken up as a topic (as Strawson actually seems to be doing in his philosophically detached discussion of what appears in the "involved" stance), but the special force of being-the-case is and must be bracketed out.

We may put the point about the force of being-the-case in another way. Whatever appears within a stance "gives itself out" as authentic, as being just what it appears as being. Even what appears as a reference "gives it-self out" as being a reference. And this is not a matter of judgment made by the stancer about the appearance; it is a matter of the appearance about which a judgment might be made. There is, then, a kind of claim or force built into the appearances in each stance (the *authenticity-claim*, as I shall call it) which is different from the status which may be ac-corded them within that very stance by the stancer. I will return to the consideration of this claim down the road a bit.

Now, it might be thought that either the thesis of migrational limitation (ii above) or the thesis of migrational freedom (iii above) is too strong. As opposed to the first, that is, the counterthesis might be proposed that (a), though some things in one stance cannot emigrate to another with-out loss of their being-the-case force, some things can preserve that force through emigration. Or it might be urged as a counterthesis to the sec-ond thesis that (b), though some things appearing in one stance can, once denuded of their being-the-case force, emigrate into another, some things, even so bereft, simply cannot.

It seems to me that such countertheses can be supported only by ap-peal to cases, but it is hard to think of any which strike one as having any but the most superficial plausibility. Strawson may be taken as providing us with examples of both, though surely he did not really intend them that way. He remarks in the first passage quoted that, in the "involved" stance, "human actions and human agents appear as the bearers of objec-tive moral properties," whereas for one in the "detached" stance "the notion of 'objective moral properties' would . . . lack significance" though "he would *observe* the prevalence of such reactions and attitudes in those around him." This suggests, on the one hand, that (a.1) human agents, or at least those human beings which have attitudes, make their appearance in full force within both stances, though they appear as differently propertied within each. It also suggests, though only by stretching things a bit, that (b.1) "objective moral properties," which straightforwardly appear in one stance, cannot even be intelligibly referred to in the other, i.e., the phrase 'objective moral property' lacks any sigificance at all in that context.

Well, as I say, I would resist being so uncharitable as to attribute either of these claims to Strawson, but the truth is that I can't frame any others which are more persuasive. In any case, it is clear that both fall flat. For, in regard to (a.1), it seems all too obvious that within the "detached" stance, at least as conceived as being profoundly opposed to the "involved," nothing ever appears as a human agent. What does appear in the "detached" stance—and might be judged to be the same thing as what appears as a human agent in the "involved" stance—appears only as an object of a non-involved sort. And, in regard to (b.1), there is, I think, a double confusion, for it is obvious both (i) that a reference is made by Strawson, and made by him as if it is significant and intelligible, in his depiction of what appears within the "detached" stance to the fact of its having-appeared-as-being-the-case in the "involved" stance that human agents are of this character and (ii) that it is simply not the case that within the "involved" stance human agents ever *appear as* the bearers of objective moral properties. The latter confusion, which I have already alluded to, would surely be the more inexcusable, though it bears more on the first counterthesis than on the second, for the notion seems to be that properties and bearers of properties, things which perhaps appear as such from the "detached" stance or some theoretical development of it, also appear as such, i.e., as bearers and properties, from the "involved" stance. But of course they don't. What Strawson may have meant to convey is that human agents in the "involved" stance appear as being such and so, which appearing could be described from another stance as being "the bearer of objective moral properties." In truth, then, nothing ever appears or could appear as a bearer of objective moral properties, for nothing can so appear in the "involved" stance and, though in the "detached" stance things may appear as bearers of properties, they cannot appear as bearers of "moral" properties. And in fact, the purported notion of "moral property" must lack significance in every stance, at least insofar as having significance involves having some conceivable application.

My general conclusion is that proposed examples of the sort of (a.1) and (b.1) are losers from the start; they attempt either to transfer a certain notion out of its sense-providing home into a context which provides no application for it or to deny the significance of a notion which, by virtue of the reference made in their very denial, they ensure.

This supposition of a sense-providing home bears further elaboration. Let me introduce it by reconsidering counterthesis (a). It seems to me that this thesis rests upon an assumption which cannot be countenanced. This assumption is that some things which appear within a stance may appear as being such and so independently of the distinctive manner in which they are regarded. But a stance cannot be intelligibly construed as being so indifferent to what appears within it. It can only be understood as a single and cohesive way of bringing into its scope whatever is illuminated or comes to light within it. This should not be taken to mean that things cannot appear within it as vagrant, as surprising or puzzling occupants of its domain of regard. But I take it that they do intrude into the landscape, even though they do so in such a manner as to appear to lack the proper papers for the place they take. They are suspicious inhabitants indeed, but inhabitants nonetheless. This allows us to see that each stance is a manner of regarding things which posits a distinctive sort of terrain or context in which what appears appears to be located. Every thing which appears is provided a home in respect to which it also appears as comfortably settled or wayward. Nothing appears *simpliciter*, all by its lonesome, completely disconnected from whatever else appears. Each thing appears in and *as being in* lodgement or habitation. The point may be put quite generally in the following way. All stances exhibit the same general structure of their manner of regard, namely, that of including the linked elements of *stancer*, *terrain*, and *inhabitants*. And counterthesis (a) overlooks this, for, by considering some things which appear within a stance as both appearing as being-the-case and yet removable without alteration from that stance and transferable to another, it is completely insensitive to the fact that any such "removal" would be forced and damaging to those things, a ripping out which would have the result of emasculating them, of sheering off their status of appearing as inhabitants of the terrain which they claim as their own.

4. I now return, as I promised, to a consideration of the authenticity-claim which is inextricable from each appearance in its home stance. I have not said, nor do I think it true, that this claim is itself distinctive or appears distinctively in each stance. What is distinctive in each stance is not this claim made by appearances, but the characters or features of that which appears under it. This may be obvious, but my reason for insisting

on it is to blunt the view, which might otherwise be put forward, that the authenticity which is claimed by an appearance within a stance is somehow that of claiming that appearance to be authentic only relative to that stance. But so far as I can discern, there is no such claim in any stance S to an authenticity-relative-to-S.

Of course, the stancer is not precluded from withholding belief or judgment about the authenticity of this or that which appears or from simply refusing to acquiesce to the claim to authenticity by some appearance. And though the *basis* of a judgment to illusion may be an intra-stance matter and that judgment may be made so as to have only an intra-stance application, it does not seem to me that the stancer ordinarily foreshortens his judgment in that way. In any case, the authenticity-claim does not itself determine the scope of a judgment of denial.

What cannot be denied, however, in any such refusal of acquiescence to the authenticity-claim of an appearance is a certain general claim, a claim regarding the *sorts* of things which are "in reality," which is embedded in the stance as such and, in that sense, stance-relative. This claim, which I will call the *reality-claim* of a specific stance S, is undeniable, unsuspendable, and even unquestionable *within* S, for if it were denied, doubted, or questioned by a stancer, it would signal the fact that that stancer is not assuming stance S in adopting such a cognitive attitude but is assuming an outside viewpoint from another stance S*. This is to say that a necessary part of what is involved in standing in any stance S is the unquestioned assumption by the stancer *qua* S-stancer of its own reality-claim.

This reality-claim is, as I have said, very general indeed. It represents only the least commissive level of acquiescence regarding the authenticity-claims of its appearances which is compatible with taking those claims seriously. The claim is that it must be the case that the things which appear within the S-terrain are representative of the sorts of things there are. It may be formulated as an assumption within S of this form:

> There are, among the things which are, things of the sort which appear as authentic in S.

It must be understood that this embedded assumption, so formulated, is *about* S and need not appear *within* S. It is not only unquestionable within S, but it is not judged within S to be true or believed by the S-stancer in any but the most generous senses of 'judged' or 'believed'. A Kantian might say that it is a necessary presupposition of the very possibility of any case of stancing of the sort S. An Aristotelian might be inclined to call it an essential structure of any case of S. I would prefer to avoid the systemic commitments which such characterizations suggest by saying that it is *constitutive of S.*

5. We need now to reconsider Strawson's picture of the two opposing stances, for we have reached a stage in our discussion where the crude distinction which he draws by use of the terms 'involved' and 'detached' is no longer very helpful.

There are two points in his characterization of the two stances which we might single out as especially disturbing. The first surfaces in his comment in the first passage quoted that, though the way reactions and attitudes appear in the "involved" stance would be alien to the "detached" stancer, "he would *observe* the prevalence of such reactions and attitudes in those around him." I have already drawn attention to a certain confusion regarding human agents which is suggested by this remark, but now I would like to note that Strawson's italicized emphasis upon the word 'observe' strongly suggests that, while the "detached" stancer makes observations, the "involved" stancer does not. The second point to be singled out is indicated by the very terms used to distinguish the two stances; one stance is that of being "involved," of being a "participant," whereas the other seems to institute a "detachment" from such involvement and the taking of an "objective" view upon it which, as he says in one place, "involves the partial or complete bracketing out or suspension of reactive feelings or moral attitudes or judgments" (40). From such expressions and remarks, one cannot help but get the impression that Strawson believes that in being "involved" one is rather thoroughly immersed in activities and concerns without any distanced or disinterested consideration of them and that, consequently, whenever one reflects upon what he is so immersed in doing he drops out of the "involvement" and falls into another and completely different stance. To put the two points together, he seems to suggest that one who is in the "involved" stance neither observes nor reflects, for to do so would be to adopt another stance entirely.

What is disturbing about such a picture, whether it is actually what Strawson had in mind or not, is that it is untrue to the character of any two stances under whatever name we wish to call them. In the first place, it is never the case that, being involved with and among things and other human agents, the stancing agent is unobservant or inattentive to any of the constituents or the situation, for if such an agent were so deeply immersed as merely to react or respond without observation or attention, he or she would simply lapse into nonagency, with the result that no stancing, no manner of regarding things, would be operative at all. The term 'observing' has a clear application to stancing in any manner of "involvement" by an agent in a situation, even if there be a *special sort* of observation or viewing which is alien to it but native to another manner of stancing. Similarly, it would be absurd to say that the stancing agent, in his or her concern for the shape of the situation and for the appropriateness of this or that action in it, cannot deliberate, consider paths and alternatives apart from one's predilections or felt attachments, or otherwise proceed reflectively and heedfully upon a certain course of action. Hence, there are also uses of such terms as 'reflecting' and 'viewing objectively' which are at home in this stance. Indeed, a case may be made for saying that a reflective phase of deliberative stancing is essential to its progress.

If this is so, and it seems inescapable, then a major problem confronting us (and Strawson as well) is to make sense out of the other, the noninvolved and nonagentive, stance as being, in some special way, detached and objective. Strawson is not very helpful about this. Sometimes he seems to have in mind what we (and Kant) might call "the theoretical stance;" sometimes he seems to suggest, not a stance at all, but a bringing to bear upon phenomena of certain theories or explanations which are of a sort to derive from science; sometimes he seems to want to invoke the rather Greek (and perhaps Spinozistic) notion of contemplation, which may well be understood in such a way as to indicate a genuine stance; and sometimes, as in the long passage I quote a few pages down, he seems to present as his "detached standpoint" something of a combination of the first two of the above, i.e., a theoretical stance which is also understood as involving the application to its appearances of a certain sort of theoretical apparatus. In truth, nothing very clear-cut comes across in his discussions regarding the character of this "standpoint." We can, I think, only conclude this much about what he has in mind. It seems to be something which is constituted by such a radical detachment or distancing as to be somehow noninvolved in essence and, since he appears to believe that it is in opposition to and thus comparable on all fours with a stance, it must be something which would count as a genuine manner of stancing.

In light of these difficulties and unclarities in Strawson's discussion of his two "standpoints," I propose to abandon use of the labels which he has given for them. I will now introduce a different and, I hope, cleaner terminology.

I propose to call any agentively involved stancing, including its own native observational and reflective dimensions and phases, *practical stancing.* As indicated in the Introduction, cases of such stancing may be said to share a structure and a determinate, though very general, manner of regard which we may refer to as *the* practical stance. This notion of a practical stance, then, is generic; it marks a genus (under the higher genus of "stance" of course) which admits of species and varieties. In addition to these, there are other species of stances, *apractical* manners of regard, which may be identified in our lives. Indeed, it would appear that any occasion of focal or intentional consciousness exemplifies some general manner of being aware of, experiencing, being directed to or concerned about, and, in a word, stancing. We may say, then, that stancing in some manner or other is ubiquitous in our lives or, at least, nearly so. So, on the practical side, we may engage in the more specialized manners of regarding things of maker (as, e.g., does the artist or craftsman), player (as, e.g., in baseball), diagnostician, strategist, technician, arranger, contriver, prudential or egoistic planner, moral agent, and so on. And on the apractical side, we may stand in the thoroughly distancing, detached, or retractive stances of the purely spectative, purely reflective, aesthetic, contemplative, or theoretical sorts. Each of these, practical and apractical, seems to require some native sensitivity or talent on the part of the stancer, as well as some development and application of such sensitivities or talents through learning and habituation, at least to the extent that the activities native to the stance are fruitfully pursued. Once established as a possibility for someone, each such stance may be, at least on some occasions, "taken" or "adopted," though one may also, on other occasions, find oneself involved in it, caught up in it, willy-nilly.

Let me now attempt to be a little more specific about what is involved in practical stancing. Any situation which is regarded practically is both taken to be and experienced as an arena of action; it is there as a setting in which a certain unspecified course of action is yet to be enacted by the agent. Any case of practical stancing continually poses to the agent the question "What shall I do?" and it calls for an answer to each such question which indicates an action which the agent may perform. Hence, to be in that stance determines both that the situation is construed as having the character of being open to alternatives of action and that the specific answer provided to each question of what to do has action-guiding significance or import. This means that, so long as one remains in the practical stance, no judgment as to what is to be done can be sufficient to determine what actually will be done. It makes no sense within the practical stance to say that some action of mine is determined to take place. It is quite consistent with this to maintain that I may judge within the practical stance that I may be compelled or fated on some occasion to move or behave in some specified fashion, but this movement or behavior cannot be seen or construed as an alternative for me as an agent; it can appear within the practical stance only as another element to be taken into account by me in considering how I might respond to the situation which includes it.

It must be emphasized that the situation which is practically regarded is itself experienced as practical in character and constitution. What this means becomes clear by the application of what has been said earlier about stances in general. Thus, that it is experienced as a whole as an arena of action determines that its elements are seen in the guise or shape of having relevance to decision and action, that is, as themselves being, at least in part, such things as paths, lures, easements, desirabilities, fulfillments, obstacles, snags, resistances, aids, instruments, materials, claims, and demands.[3] Moreover, the things one experiences appear as being so practically cast or molded and, in such appearance, as authentic and fully real on their own. Of course, for something to appear as such is not necessarily for it to be judged or accepted as really being such by the stancing agent. Some degree of practical assessment of the situation and the way things appear in it will constitute part of what is involved in attempting to determine what to do. But the general character of the arena as practical cannot be disavowed or judged irrelevant. Therefore, the practically stancing agent is committed—so long, that is, as he remains in the practical stance—to the general claim that there are things of a sort which are practical in their very nature. It is a constitutive reality-claim of any occasion of practical stancing that there are, among the things which are, things of a distinctively practical cast.[4]

Since Kant it has been common to contrast the practical stance with the theoretical. If we are careful about this, the comparison can be illuminating. We need to remind ourselves that the items compared lie at different levels of generality and that they are not exhaustive of stances which may be compared. But though the theoretical stance is not the only apractical or retractive manner of stancing, it is one which ontologists and other philosophers often take to constitute their manner of approach. So conceived, it is of special interest to us here.

The first point which might be made regarding a purported theoretical stance is that, as a *stance*, it is not to be identified with the theoretical *enterprise*, though certain practitioners of that enterprise may employ a certain theoretical manner of stancing in certain of its phases. A theoretical enterprise is not itself a stance but a process of investigation which aims at a system or theory in terms of which, supposedly, a certain sort of understanding or explanation can be given of a designated subject-matter, and certain questions which have arisen about that subject-matter can be answered. Still, it seems reasonable to assume that a theoretical stance, in order to live up to its name, will be widely accepted as having some relevance to theory and theoretical understanding. The explanation of this, I think, is just that how things appear in it is often taken as preliminary to theoretical proposal or as providing the appropriate arrangement of confirming or disconfirming material for the testing of proposed theories.

A second point of clarification involves the recognition that such a stance is not to be identified either with mere reflection as it may arise in a variety of different stances or with a broader and overviewing sort of reflective consideration which may be adopted in the comparison of stances. I will come back to a consideration of this latter sort of reflection in a subsequent section.

Given these strictures, how may we identify and characterize the so-called theoretical stance? The key, I think, lies in two aspects of it, namely, the radical extent of its distancing and the sort of terrain of inhabitants which that distancing institutes. An abbreviated formula for this may be derived from consideration of the stancer-terrain-inhabitants structure of any stance. In contrast to the specification of the structure of practical stancing as that of *agent-arena of action-things* (introducing here a specialized use of the latter term), the structure of the theoretical stance may be specified as that of *subject-field-objects.* The idea is that the stancer in its role of subject is so radically removed from its terrain of regard as to be, in principle, incapable of appearing within it in any stancing role, whether as agent, viewer, inquirer, reflecter, perceiver, or subject. It goes along with this that the terrain is posited as a field which is populated by "things" which stand over against the subject as oppositions, "objections," to it. Whereas the agent-stancer must inhabit the arena of action and stand in citizenship with the things which also inhabit it, the subject-stancer cannot have a place in its field, cannot assume or be taken as assuming the status of an object, and cannot be characterized or taken as presupposed by means of any of the ingredients, relations, or features which serve to characterize those very objects which appear only on its presupposition. And though other agents and stancers than the stancing agent may appear in or be taken to have a place in an arena of action, nothing can appear as an agent, subject, or stancer of any sort in a field of objects.

From this it is clear that no more striking opposition to practical stancing can be found than the theoretical, for the latter assumes a reality-claim, namely, that there are, among the things which are, things which are of the object sort, which posits entities of a sort which incorrigibly resist any practical cast or character. And on the other side, the things claimed by the practical stance would be incapable of being mere objects. Still, the two reality-claims, being of the minimal scope they are, are not contradictory, for it would remain open that the ultimate sorts of "things which are" are irreducibly diverse. Of course, the totality of real things would, on such an account, have to constitute a collection or multiplicity within which there obtained an unbridgeable gulf. If this radical dualism is unacceptable as a view of what is, and surely it must be, then one or both of these reality-claims must be untrue as it stands. It remains, however, a possibility that each can be honored to a lesser extent by appeal to a general constitution of things which allows that these things have aspects or faces which are such that one preserves practical cast and another, taken in abstraction, achieves the status of an object. But these considerations, arising naturally in our reflection upon the two stances, take us far into ontology.

6. This introduces the basic theme of this chapter, namely, the ground of ontological interest. My reason for bringing up stances in the first place has been to make the points (1) that, upon our reflective consideration of them, we become aware, however vaguely and intuitively at first, of the difference between them in regard to the distinctiveness of their appearances and their reality-claims and (2) that, once we have reflected upon what is involved in those claims, we can put each of them to the question of whether it is true or not. And this is not all. For (3), in putting the claims of *different* stances to the question, we find ourselves in the position of attempting to adjudicate between them or of finding a way of construing reality which will somehow present a basis for accepting all of them as, if not true as they stand, acceptable in part. The drive toward system begins as soon as we see the desirability of having a comprehensive and coherent view of reality in terms of which an assessment of these claims can be made. So it is that the initial ground of our ontological interest lies in those ways of orienting ourselves which are commissive in regard to reality, i.e., in our lived and everyday manners of stancing. All that is needed beyond this is the move of reflection and the questioning which comes along with it.

It is common to find in philosophical discussions another view. This is that the entire project of ontology depends upon the invocation by some philosophers of an intuition or insight about the supposed significance of questions about "reality in general" which comes from outside of everyday life and has no clear application to it. On this view, philosophers who claim to be doing ontology *impose* the "question of reality" upon appearances. Thus, ontology becomes ungrounded except by reference to the special privilege which some philosophers, bewitched perhaps by language or a desire for importance and the appearance of profundity, claim as their own. Worse, the very *meaningfulness* of ontological concern becomes suspect and the purported reference to a special subject-matter tenuous and obscure. The long history of ontological interest and inquiry among many of our avowedly greatest and most reflective philosophers becomes thereby mysterious and, in the final analysis, embarrassing.

My aim has been to show that this externalist view of how ontological interest always or must arise is simply mistaken. Not only may its ground lie in our everyday affairs and concerns, but the meaningfulness of questions about reality derives from the simple fact that claims about reality, however often left unexamined in our daily lives, are engrained into its most radical, its most primary and rooted, ways of regarding things. Reference to "reality" is not a bolt from the blue, so to speak, but an awareness and honoring of something which we seem quite unable to avoid, namely, our turning toward things in our attempt to make sense out of them, to give them their due, and to divine our proper way among them.

7. We come back now to Strawson's attempt to undermine the legitimacy of the question he poses, for, if he is right about this, the legitimacy of the sorts of questions which I have proposed above may also be thought to require reconsideration. The reader will recall that, after distinguishing his two "standpoints," he puts the question like this:

> How natural it is, then, to ask the question: "Which is the correct standpoint? Which is the standpoint from which we see things as they really are?" (36)

But before proceeding to consider his response to this question, we might note three things about how he poses it.

First, however misbegotten or naive the question may be, it is, he says, "natural" to raise it. This seems right. I have not argued that by virtue of merely reflecting upon our diverse stances we are ever likely to phrase what strikes us as significant in regard to reality in a philosophically sophisticated or acceptably precise way. The initial *arousal* of ontological interest requires only a respectable ground to be significant; it needs precision of statement only for the furtherance of ontological inquiry.

Second, it is clear from Strawson's manner of introducing the question that it follows upon a reflective consideration of the diversity among at least two of our stances. It is important to see that it cannot arise within either stance, for if it did it could not be posed as neutral to them. One might think it somehow derives from the "detached" stance, but to construe it in this way would be to beg the question in favor of or, if the question be spurious, in disfavor of that stance. And it is clear from Strawson's own response to the question that this is not his reading of it.

Third, the question is a mess after all and for two general reasons. It is loaded; it rests upon the presupposition that one of two stances reveals things correctly and the other reveals things incorrectly. But it is patent that these are not the only two stances and that we must in any case entertain the possibility at the beginning that neither may be entirely "correct." A less naive question would be whether we "see things" correctly from either one of the stances. The second reason for balking at the question as Strawson frames it is that it is a question to which we already have a ready answer. For only the most credulous of persons would simply acquiesce to the authenticity-claims of all of the appearances in any stance in which one stands at any time or during any interval. The only claim which it is reasonable to find at issue would be the reality-claim, which does not raise for us the question of whether we "see things as they really are" within a certain stance, but whether there are any things of that sort. And this question is, I have argued, quite in order. Call it the *reality-claim question*. It has the form: Is the reality-claim of stance S true?

Now to Strawson's own response.

> I want to say that the appearance of contradiction arises only if we assume the existence of some metaphysically absolute standpoint from which we can judge between the two standpoints I have been contrasting. But there is no such superior standpoint—or none that we know of; it is the idea of such a standpoint that is the illusion. Once that illusion is abandoned, the appearance of contradiction is dispelled. We can recognize, in our conception of the real, a reasonable relativity to standpoints that we do know and can occupy. Relative to the standpoint which we normally occupy as social beings, prone to moral and personal reactive attitudes, human actions, or some of them, are morally toned and propertied in the diverse ways signified in our rich vocabulary of moral appraisal. Relative to the detached naturalistic standpoint which we can sometimes occupy, they have no properties but those which can be described in the vocabularies of naturalistic analysis and explanation (including, of course, psychological analysis and explanation). (38)

In view of these remarks, we might say that, in general, Strawson's view is that, since our question could be *answered* only from a superior standpoint and since no such standpoint exists, it follows that our question cannot be answered. I think he might want to go on to say that a question that cannot in principle be answered is an illegitimate question.

This response is worth a moment's puzzlement. I have pointed out that Strawson *raises* the question from a reflective "standpoint" which must be distinguished from the two stances under comparison. He makes no claim, nor do I, that this third stance or "standpoint" is such as to provide the means for answering the question. But it seems just as reasonable to

me to accept a question as significant because it is raised from a legitimate "standpoint" as to deny the significance of the question because
there is no "superior standpoint" from which it can be answered.

Yet it is also clear from this passage that Strawson offers something
which looks like an answer. Or rather, he makes a stance-relative proposal, as we may call it, in terms of which the illegitimate question can
be transformed into a legitimate one and then provided with an affirmative answer. It comes to this. Since there is a stance S^* within which the
reality-claim of stance S would be false, since there is no superior standpoint available to us from which we can decide between S and S^*, but
since, "in our conception of the real," there is a "relativity to standpoints," then we can conclude that "relative to the standpoint" of stance S
its reality-claim is true. Thus, to the question "Is the reality-claim of S, understood as a claim of what is real relative to S, true?" the answer is "yes."
What can we make of this?

It is not altogether clear in this passage exactly what it is which we are
to take as "relative to standpoint." We might note, to begin, that there is
one way of deciding this which would not serve to transform the question after all. On this reading, it is the relevant *claim* regarding what is
real, as well as the *picture or conception* of the real, which is to be taken
as stance-relative. Thus, the reality-claim of practical stancing is a claim
which is *of* practical stancing and not *of* a theoretical view of things. But,
of course, the reality-claim question is not one which asks for the circumstances under which we buy into this claim or conception, but whether
the claim or conception which we buy into under the circumstances of
stance S is true. In other words, the assumption that the reality-claim at
issue is itself stance-relative in this way is a presupposition of the question as we originally put it forward. Surely this is not what Strawson had
in mind.

There is, however, another reading which might be made of the
phrase "our conception of the real" in the last passage. We might take
Strawson as indicating, not that each stance includes a distinctive picture
of what is real, but that it employs a special concept of "the real," a concept such that the word 'real', when used to invoke it, must always be
taken to have a stance-relative sense. On this reading, Strawson would,
indeed, find our reality-claim question conceptually incomplete or perhaps systematically ambiguous. But a consequence of this is that he must
fail to take the reality-claim of a stance for what it is. It is not a claim to
something being real-relative-to-the-stancing or real-relative-to-S or real-
in-a-special-S-sense; it is simply a claim to something being real. To think
otherwise is simply to fail to see the claim for what it is as it arises and is
accepted within a stance.

There is more to be said against the view we get on this reading. It would be self-defeating, I would think, to maintain that whenever we use the word 'real', whatever we may think we mean by it, it is *really* the case that we are using it in some sense which is relative to a specific manner of stancing. On what picture of "the real" could that be taken to be "really" the case? There may not be, as Strawson would say, a "superior standpoint" at which we can stand, view the world as it is, and divine which, if any, inferior "standpoint" best reveals "the real." But neither, then, is there a superior "standpoint" from which one can see that neither of two "profoundly opposed standpoints" reveals things as they are but only discloses things which are taken to be real in a sense of 'real' relative to that *"standpoint."* His own ontological stand could only be accepted as justified, it seems to me, by appeal to such a "superior standpoint." Given, then, that there is no such "standpoint" or stance to which he does or can appeal, then his argument for a stance-relative sense of 'real' (if that is his view) can hardly be taken seriously.

Our reality-claim questions survive these "no superior standpoint" and "stance-relativity" objections to their significance and legitimacy. Still, someone might object that, even though the *raising* of such questions is a significant and "natural" act, the questions *themselves* cannot be countenanced as significant, for to be significant a question must be such that there are some means available for correctly answering it and with regard to these "questions" there are no such means at all. The point cannot be, of course, that, in order for a "yes" or "no" question to be significant, we must have available to us *conclusive* evidence or reasons for either a "yes" or "no" answer, for we do not expect such conclusiveness for most of our questions, nor do we assume that conclusive evidence or reasons are in principle always discoverable. The point must be that, in order for such a question to be significant, there must be, at least in principle, some available evidence or reasons which can count as being genuine evidence for or reasons for one answer rather than another. I don't know why we should assume this. In any case, it is hardly obvious that there can be no means, no available considerations, which might warrant our taking one answer rather than another as correct. We must remember that the questions at issue arise upon reflective consideration of diverse stances. What basis could there be for excluding further reflective considerations as genuine and appropriate reasons for accepting or denying the reality-claim of *S*? It might, of course, be argued that, given that reflection involves the taking of a stance or "standpoint" in its own right, no apparent evidence within it can ever be anything but stance-relative and hence biased. But this argument self-destructs. For, apart from reflection we cannot even distinguish stances, their reality-claims, and their distinctive manners of regard, nor could we then make any sense of evidence or reasons being stance-relative. If apparent evidence derived from reflection on this score cannot be accepted as genuine evidence, then our own, as well as Strawson's, identification of *different* stances goes down the drain. The question "Are there different stances?" would be, on this count, just as illegitimate as the reality-claim question. But then the general point that such evidence, because it is derived within a stance, cannot be accepted as genuine evidence must go down the drain as well. This does not, of course, indicate that reflective consideration of any stance S will in fact provide evidence or reasons which incline me to answer the reality-claim question regarding S one way rather than the other. It is only to say that the possibility is not ruled out in principle.

8. There is one further point about the reality-claim question which I think it important to consider in this chapter. There is an approach to the question which appears to take it seriously, but which in the end does not, for, again, it does not take the radical diversity of stances for what they are. This approach can be illustrated by considering some remarks by J. L. Mackie. He introduces the issue as follows:

> I conclude, then, that ordinary moral judgements include a claim to objectivity, an assumption that there are objective values in just the sense in which I am concerned to deny this. And I do not think it is going too far to say that this assumption has been incorporated in the basic, conventional, meanings of moral terms. Any analysis of the meanings of moral terms which omits this claim to objective, intrinsic, prescriptivity is to that extent incomplete . . . (35)

> The claim to objectivity, however ingrained in our language and thought, is not self-validating. It can and should be questioned. But the denial of objective values will have to be put forward not as the result of an analytic approach, but as an "error theory," a theory that although most people in making moral judgements implicitly claim, among other things, to be pointing to something objectively prescriptive, these claims are all false. (35)

It appears from this that the sort of claim to "objectivity" (a term which Mackie consistently misuses) which is under consideration is much the same as one which we may attribute to the moral species of practical stancing. Unfortunately, Mackie says nothing about stances or how things appear in them; rather, he finds the claim to be "included" in ordinary

moral judgments or perhaps, to be a bit more charitable to his inten-
tions, in our making of moral judgments in ordinary affairs. For this reason, it is not at all clear that he is attentive to how things appear experientially, so to speak, when we open ourselves to them in a moral or
otherwise practical manner. But we can adapt Mackie's remarks to our
purpose perhaps by considering the position that there is a species of
practical stancing which is "moral" at least partially by virtue of the facts
that (i) things appear within it as both having or somehow exhibiting
"moral values" and as claiming their own authenticity and that (ii) it is
claimed by it that, though many or at least some of these appearances
may not be authenticating after all, there are things which have or exhibit
"objective values" in the world. It would follow from this analysis that any
attempt to undermine the claim in (ii), to deny its truth—as seems to be
Mackie's goal—would be at the same time an attempt to undermine the
moral stance, to deny its applicability to the world as it really is, and thus
to establish that stance as a systematically misleading manner of orientation to the world.

Now I wish to allow that Mackie is correct in seeing the issue as an ontological one. For, if one, in reflecting upon the moral stance, questions
the truth of its reality-claim, then that person is expressing an interest,
not just in the appearance of things, but in reality and what is to be included in it. But if Mackie starts out right, he soon gets off track. Mackie
proceeds in his attempt to undermine the reality-claim of moral stancing
by simply begging the question in favor of another stance.

Consider these two passages in which he indicates what he has called
the "queerness" of moral sorts of things:

> If there were objective values, then they would be entities or qual-
> ities or relations of a very strange sort, utterly different from any-
> thing else in the universe. Correspondingly, if we were aware of
> them, it would have to be by some special faculty of moral per-
> ception or intuition, utterly different from our ordinary ways of
> knowing everything else. (38)

> It would make a radical difference to our metaphysics if we had to
> find room for objective values—perhaps something like Plato's
> Forms—somewhere in our picture of the world. (24)

Now the fact that "objective values" would be "utterly different from
anything else in the universe" may be taken as trivially true. But that they
would be of a "very strange sort" hardly follows, unless one already has
committed himself to such an intolerant picture of the things which be-

long in the world that they would not or could not "fit in." And one must suppose that it would be very difficult, perhaps even impossible, to "find room" for such moral things in what appears to be Mackie's own theoretically purified and, indeed, more narrowly scientifically construed picture of the world. Surely this is not surprising. But surely it is obvious as well that in the "picture of the world," if this phrase is appropriate, which we assume in our everyday practical stancing, the problem of "making room" for such things does not arise. Such entities are already there. Moreover, they are experienced as being there, so that we need not, in order to be aware of them, invoke some "special faculty of moral perception or intuition" which is "utterly different from our ordinary ways of knowing everything else." If there is some special manner of construing things which is invoked, surely it is Mackie who invokes it, for practical stancing, even in its moral variety, is as ordinary as rain, whereas the manner of construing things which Mackie makes use of is extraordinary indeed and one which requires a certain use of the theoretical stance which has not only to be learned, but can only be acquired with some effort and patience.

If this sort of "reasoning by bias" were not so common today, I would not dwell on it, for it was well-diagnosed by the ancient Skeptics. I will come back to the Skeptics' formulation of the mistake which is involved in a moment, but let me first give another example of it in recent literature.

The following appears in a book by Gilbert Harman.

> . . . observation plays a role in science that it does not seem to play in ethics. The difference is that you need to make assumptions about certain physical facts to explain the occurrence of the observations that support a scientific theory, but you do not seem to need to make assumptions about any moral facts to explain the occurrence of the so-called moral observations I have been talking about. In the moral case, it would seem that you need only make assumptions about the psychology or moral sensibility of the person making the moral observation. In the scientific case, theory is tested against the world. (6)

The point of this so-called "best explanation" move is, it seems, to undermine our need or predilection to assume "moral facts." But this is just confused. We need only point out that there is a very good reason to accept *within moral stancing* the reality-claim of moral stancing, namely, that we must do so in order to be engaged upon moral stancing at all. It is, of course, obvious that this reason both has its home in a certain moral context and derives its force as a good reason from that context. It is equally obvious that it may not be thought to be a good reason from outside that context; it is clearly not thought to have any force from the theoretical point of view of one who, like Harman, assumes a certain explanatory test of what is to count as real. But what does this show? Only that what we have good reason to accept within one stance may be something which we can find no good reason to accept within another. And apart from some further argument to the effect that one stance deserves priority over the other as a reliable access to reality, no justification for preferring the reasons of one over the reasons of the other can be given.

Now, as I have said, the later Skeptics take account of the botched sort of reasoning involved here. In the first four of the ten modes of suspension of judgment, as Sextus presents them, we confront a variety of situations in which things appear differently to different viewers. Sextus' first move in each of these modes is to identify such oppositions and to set out apparently conflicting cases. The general form for doing this may be represented as follows:[5]

(1) x appears as F relative to S, and
(2) x appears as F^* relative to S^*.

His next move is to identify a certain sort of mistaken attempt to avoid that apparent balance or equality of credibility between (1) and (2) which purportedly results in suspension of judgment. The balance to be achieved may be expressed as follows:

(3) There is no basis for deciding between the claims of S and S^*.

And the particular sort of mistake which Sextus exposes may be expressed like this:

(4) It is not acceptable to decide between the claims of S and S^* from or within either S or S^*.

This sort of mistake is obvious and hardly needs belaboring. It is the familiar spoiler of begging the question. Sextus indicates his scorn for it in his discussion of the second mode, i.e., the mode which contrasts appearances relative to different human beings, as follows:

> Now the dogmatists are a rather conceited class of people, and they say that they must give themselves the preference over other men in the matter of judging things; but we know that their claim

is absurd because they themselves form a party to the disagree-
ment. Furthermore, if they are thus prejudiced in favour of themselves whenever they judge appearances, then they are begging
the question before they even begin their judgment, because they
are turning the decision over to themselves. (56–57)

It is, however, the fourth mode which comes closest to providing an
application of this diagnosis to stances. In this mode Sextus considers the
different opposing "states" in which one may find oneself, e.g., healthy or
unhealthy, sleeping or waking, hungry or satiated, drunk or sober, afraid
or confident. The mistake of begging the question is applied: ". . . the fact
of his being in some state or other while attempting to pass judgment
will make him a party to the controversy . . ." (61). We have only to adapt
the reference to diverse states to include those of the even more radical "circumstances" of diverse stances to make the simple point I have
brought in criticism of Mackie and Harman.

One further observation regarding Sextus' analysis must be made. It is
clear that (4) does not entail (3), nor does it appear that Sextus meant to
claim that it did.[6] The acceptance of (4) does not preclude the possibility
that some other, non-question-begging basis for deciding between S and
S^* might be found. Moreover, the issue need not be that of deciding between them, but of favoring or giving more weight to one or the other.
Of course, the Skeptics do not think that such a basis for either deciding
between or favoring is likely to be found. But here, I think, they have
gone too far.

9. There is one sort of reply which might be made to my diagnosis of
the procedure of Mackie and Harman as question-begging. It may be put
like this. The question of the truth or falsity of the reality-claim of moral
(or practical) stancing is itself ontological and therefore a theoretical
one; it is not a question which arises within moral stancing but only from
without and from a theoretical stance. Therefore, it calls for a theoretical
answer. Thus, a theoretical assessment of its explanatory value is precisely what is called for in order to answer it.

But this picture is misdrawn from the beginning. We must allow, of
course, that the question "Is the reality-claim of moral stancing true?" is
one which does not arise, at least in any ordinary circumstances, within
moral stancing. One can, it seems, raise the question only upon reflecting on moral stancing and, through reflective consideration, by the focusing of interest on the reality-claim involved. And we may well allow that
such reflective viewing is, of itself, neither moral nor practical in its concern, for it raises a question of truth rather than one of action or obli-

gation. So much may be allowed, but nothing follows from this which could be construed as favoring the relevance of the theoretical.

For, in the first place, though the reflective questioning of the reality-claim or moral stancing is not a moral questioning, neither is it theoretical. To assume that it is would be to assimilate a question of the form "Is such and such true?" to one of the form "How is so and so to be theoretically understood or explained?" In our own case, the reality-claim question would have to be understood as implicitly raising something like the question "What is the correct explanation of why the reality-claim of moral stancing is incorrigible in that context and is it, on that explanation, to be accepted, rejected, or left undecided?" But our question is not this one but the much simpler and more straightforward one which asks whether—apart from whatever reasons, moral, theoretical, or otherwise, we might have for deciding one way or the other—a certain claim is true.

But, second, neither does it call for or accept as a legitimate *sort* of answer only one which derives from or is based upon theoretical considerations. The question is, if taken seriously, an open question in the sense that it allows the legitimacy, the appropriateness, of either of two answers, no matter the source of one's conviction. At the same time, however, it does refer, by virtue of its very formulation, to at least one answer that has been given, namely, the "yes" answer indicated by the fact that the affirmative claim is actually made within moral stancing. That is, the question is conceived from the beginning as one to which moral stancing provides a straightforward, even if perhaps incorrect, answer. Thus, it cannot in consistency be conceived as a question for which only an answer derived from some nonmoral stance or basis is to be taken as a proper *sort* of answer.

And finally, the reflective questioning at issue cannot be taken to indicate, of itself, any preference for a theoretical method or procedure— nor even a practical or distinctively reflective one—for correctly answering whatever questions it poses. Of course, nothing in this precludes either one's further reflection upon the various proposals which have been offered for answering it or one's further reflective consideration of the evidence or reasons which may be offered in favor of one answer or the other. Nor is it precluded that, upon reflective consideration of various proposals and reasons, one will find oneself inclined to give one answer rather than the other, come to believe or accept an answer, or even conclude that such a belief is warranted by the reflectively available evidence. But nothing in any of this goes any way towards providing any initial or built-in encouragement for favoring theory, theoretical stancing, or theoretical considerations.

My conclusion, then, stands. Any judgment to the effect that a nontheoretical construal of reality can be set aside in favor of a theoretical construal cannot be supported *merely* by showing that the nontheoretical construal is not theoretically satisfactory. To assume so is as good an example of begging the question as one can find.

10. Given, then, that there are at least two manners of stancing (but surely more) which are in opposition both in respect to their native appearances and terrain and in respect to their reality-claims, and given that these claims are not self-validating and that there is no superior "standpoint" or stance within which reality can be surveyed and made available for the purpose of deciding between these claims, it would seem that we can have no firm grounds for simply dismissing either reality-claim out of hand. It would appear to be the way of wisdom, then, as we carry our questioning into ontological investigation, to remain open and to proceed on the *hypothesis* that each manner of stancing has at least some limited measure or scope of legitimacy as an access to reality. In such a way we would take each manner of stancing seriously as representing diverse and illuminating ways of orienting ourselves to the world and the things in it. Of course, we must allow that, in spite of our openness, it remains a possibility that the general picture of the world which we derive from practical stancing and, hence, from moral stancing is simply mistaken. And for the same reason we can say the same of any theoretical picture, whether scientific, historical, philosophical, or whatever.

On the other hand, our adopting an ontological openness to both manners of stancing must not be taken to preclude our being inclined, upon reflective consideration of each, to favor one over the other as providing access to the way things are, so long, that is, as such favor does not carry over into exclusivity. What such favor might come to, however, and how it might be supported are issues which lead us beyond a consideration of the grounds of ontological interest and into considerations regarding the nature of the ontological enterprise and its proper path.

2

Ontological Systems

♦♦♦ 1. I have proposed a sketch of the ontological enterprise as a process which is bounded by the domain of ontological interest at one pole and the achievement of its aim, a comprehensive and acceptable system, at the other. Having considered the former pole in the previous chapter, we may now consider the latter. The issues before us, then, are (i) the nature of the system at which the ontologist aims and (ii) the conditions on its acceptability. Once we have reached a general understanding of these matters we shall then be enabled to move with better footing in the two following chapters to a consideration of the process of inquiry and construction which lies between these poles.

2. As indicated in the introduction, the sort of system about which we are concerned will be one which is constructed with the aim of being true of reality. With this in mind, the following general observations regarding the constraints upon such a system appear warranted. In the subsequent sections of this chapter I will attempt to provide a bit more detail.

(1) Given a particular system S_1, it is part of what is involved in claiming that it is an ontological system that a claim may be made of the form

$$S_1 \text{ is true of } R,$$

where R designates the subject-matter of ontological concern, i.e., reality.[7] A claim of this sort, which I shall call the *R-claim* of the relevant system, is metasystemic *relative to* the system about which it is a claim.[8] It is an assumption of the ontological enterprise that no system can be such as to be both an ontological system and inclusive of every possible R-claim. Thus, the notion of "system" which is involved is that of something about which metasystemic claims can be made.

(2) But, similarly, metasystemic claims may be made in regard to systems of universal science. Given such a proposed system S_2, one may claim

S_2 is comprehensively applicable to every item in L
or
S_2 is explanatory of every theory of a domain of L,

where L refers to the totality of whatever arises within our lives. These are examples of what might be called L-claims.

Now it is important to realize that the ontological enterprise has as its goal the construction of a system about which both an R-claim and some such L-claims can be made. But there is a logical difference in the status of such claims as they may be made in behalf of such a system. An R-claim is, we might say, a condition upon the truth of the claim that a system is an *ontological* one. L-claims are not. However much some such L-claims may be necessary conditions on a system's being considered as a system of universal science, they are not thus determinative of an ontology. But in spite of this, it would appear that the making of some such L-claims constitutes a condition on any claim to the *acceptability* of an ontological system among those who legitimately engage upon the ontological enterprise. Or to put the point in another way, it is a goal of the ontological enterprise not merely to come up with a system which is true of reality, but one which meets certain conditions for the acceptability of the claim that that system is true of reality. And among such acceptability conditions (A-conditions) it would appear that some consist of the truth of certain L-claims. Thus:

For any x, x is an ontological system if and only if (i) x is a genuine system and (ii) an R-claim is made about x.

For any x, x is an acceptable ontological system if and only if (i) x is an ontological system and (ii) the proper acceptability conditions are satisfied by x.

(3) This allows us to distinguish three sorts of conditions which may be invoked in the consideration of a proposed ontological system. There are

> S-conditions, i.e., conditions on something's being a system,
> O-conditions, i.e., conditions on a system's having the status of being ontological, and
> A-conditions, i.e., conditions on an ontological system's acceptability in the ontological enterprise.

Consideration of these conditions lead us from the consideration of the nature of systems to the consideration, in turn, of the nature of ontological systems, the criteria for adjudication among rival ontological systems, and the nature and methodology of the ontological enterprise. The concerns of this chapter thereby lead into those of the next.

(4) A proposed system of universal science may also be proposed (given the addition of an R-claim) as an ontological system. Thus it is that there can be nothing intrinsic to a system *per se* which may enable us to determine whether it is to be taken as an ontological system or a system of universal science. The distinction between ontology and universal science cannot be made out systemically alone, at least not in all cases. (It is conceivable that there are O-conditions regarding the *structure* of the system which need not apply to universal science.) Thus, to be provided merely with a set of categories and principles which comprise a system of supposed universal applicability is not to be provided with sufficient evidence to determine whether or not an ontology is in the offing. One must look to the larger extrasystemic context for the grounds for making such a decision. Is Leibniz' monadology an ontological theory or merely a sort of pre-Kantian attempt at universal science? Is Frege's supposed "ontology" ontology in fact? Is Whitehead's categoreal scheme of *Process and Reality* an attempt merely at a sort of universal science after all? We can answer *these* questions, sure enough. But there are harder cases to be found among lesser thinkers.

It seems that we need to consider this issue of the separability of the systemic and extrasystemic in more detail. I will make an attempt at this in the next section.

(5) Of S-conditions *per se* I shall have little to say here, for, on the whole, what might be meant by saying that a product of theoretical investigation realizes the status of a genuine system cannot be clearly made out except by means of the more general consideration of the variety of conceptual structures which serve the purpose of providing for the un-

derstanding and the determination of the significance of things, entities, materials, or whatever. Systems comprise only one possible sort of such conceptual structures; they are precisely those which are contrived for the purpose of achieving "systematic" understanding. There are, it seems clear, other forms of understanding than that provided by theoretical investigation and there are therefore other means of gaining understanding than the employment of systems.

What does a "systematic" understanding of something come to? It seems to me to involve at least this much. There is (a) the specification of a general subject-matter which is articulated in some general fashion; there is (b) the provision of a framework or schema of specified entities or other items, together with a specification of order among them; there is (c) the interpretation of this schema in terms of the sorts of articulations of the subject-matter; and there is (d) the application of the interpreted schema to a particular case or cases of the subject-matter. In view of this, a system may be said to provide an interpreted schema, i.e., both (b) and (c), for understanding something by means of the assignment of that something to a position which is allowed for it in the schema considered as a whole. For this sort of understanding the schema is exhaustive; no trait of the thing to be understood is to be taken as unassimilable to the schema or, if it is, then that thing is to be taken, from the point of view of the system, to be unintelligible or inexplicable in that respect. Such a schema may also be said to provide for the significance of any entity or articulation which falls within its scope, for the only "importance" of such an entity relative to the system is precisely that of being such as to be assignable to some position in the schema. From the point of view of a system an entity is intelligible only as a *case*.

What is applied to anything which may be articulated in a particular case of the subject-matter is the system itself under a certain interpretation. There are two guiding conditions, then, for the shape such a system must take; namely, it must conform to the articulable things of a specified subject-matter and it must be so structured as to fulfill the aims of applicability. In view of this, what can we say about its minimal structural conditions? Very little I am afraid. Apart from the specification of the subject-matter and a certain articulation of it, one cannot be entirely comfortable in appealing to one structural model rather than another. Clearly, quantities, qualities, relations, individuals, and sorts move us in different directions and suggest different forms of ordering relationships. But perhaps this much might be said. A system must have at least three components, each of which is primitive relative to the system itself, namely, a set of terms, a set of principles which serve to determine the ordering relationships among these terms, and a set of principles for interpreting those terms. The specification of the appropriate structure of ontological systems, as we shall see in a moment, causes special difficulties.

These remarks, abstract as they are, have an important consequence for our own eventual investigation into the structure of the practical arena. Such an order cannot be articulated in its own native applicability as a system, for the point of such an order is not the achievement of a "systematic" but a practical understanding. If a system is to be applied to the practical arena, it can only be by means of moving from a "presystematic" to a "systematic" level of consideration, by means, that is, of the application of a structure derived from another climate of concern and devoted to a different conception of understanding and significance.

3. We may now turn to a more careful consideration of the appropriate constituents of an ontological system, the roles in regard to these of the R-claim and certain other metasystemic and extrasystemic statements, and, in respect to the last, A-conditions in general. It is useful to begin by puzzling a bit about the general distinction between systemic and extrasystemic claims.

We may make a start by considering a distinction between types of metaphysical statement proposed by William A. Christian in regard to Whitehead's metaphysics.

> To see what sorts of truth-claims are made in Whitehead's speculative philosophy, we should begin by distinguishing his categoreal scheme . . . and its systematic development from the pre-systematic and post-systematic statements in which the scheme is, so to speak, embedded.
>
> By pre-systematic statements I mean statements of facts Whitehead means to take account of and do justice to in his speculative construction, for example:

> All things flow.
> Consciousness presupposes experience.
> There are many things.
> . . . . .

> We might characterize these statements by saying that neither their logical subjects nor their predicates are expressed by terms taken from Whitehead's own categoreal scheme. Instead, their terms are taken from ordinary usage, from science, from religious discourse, or from traditional philosophical usage, and have the meanings they are given in those contexts. Such terms may be called non-systematic terms . . .

By systematic statements I mean statements of relationships within the scheme, for example:

A prehension has a subject, a datum, and a subjective form.
Eternal objects are ingredient in actual entities.
. . . . .

In statements of this sort, all the terms are derived from the categoreal scheme. Both the logical subjects and the predicates of these statements are expressed by systematic terms.

By post-systematic statements I mean statements in which facts and principles of various sorts are interpreted in terms of the categoreal scheme, for example:

The finite things that endure through time are not actual entities but nexus of actual entities.
. . . . .

In these statements some of the terms are non-systematic terms and some are systematic terms. And the point of the statements is to put the facts and principles expressed by the non-systematic terms into a certain perspective. The systematic terms are used to interpret non-systematic terms (Christian 74–75).

This is a good beginning and a very useful way of approaching Whitehead's *Process and Reality*, which is pretty dense as it stands. But there are difficulties. (Please note that, when referring to Christian's own view, I shall continue to use his terms 'pre-systematic', 'systematic', and 'post-systematic', but when, after a critical look at it, I return to my own exposition, I shall revert to the use of the root 'systemic'. From then on I shall speak of the "presystemic," "postsystemic," "transsystemic," and so on. This language is, I think, more apt; in any case the distinctions it signals cut along somewhat different lines.)

On Christian's tripartition, the form of the three sorts of statement may be symbolized as follows, using lowercase letters for non-systematic terms and capital letters for the systematic ones:

pre-systematic: . . . *ab* . . .
systematic: . . . *AB* . . .
post-systematic: . . . *aB* . . .

Looked at like this, the division is exhaustive and lucid. But in several ways it tends to obscure matters of importance which have to do with diverse functions among claims which arise within each of these three divisions. For the time being we may confine our attention to a division of function among statements of the general form indicated for post-systematic statements.

In the first place, Christian's notion of post-systematic statements is ambiguous between statements which are the product of the application of the system and those which provide the means for that application. One can't just apply the scheme at will, as he feels like it. A sort of Kantian schematism is required in order to determine the proper application of the categories. Such a schematism must consist of rules which, in order to bridge the gap between the systematic and the non-systematic use of language, contain terms of both sorts. They are, that is, something like rules of translation, though it is probably more revealing to think of them as rules of interpretation for the constituents of systematic statements.

On this view, then, there are at least two possible sorts of post-systematic statements, those which serve as rules of interpretation and those which may be generated by their means. The relation between the two may be illustrated by reference to the following inference form (using lowercase and capital letters as before):

Rule of interpretation:	All a's are to be taken as A's.
Pre-systematic claim:	This (all, some) b is an a.
Generated claim:	This (all, some) b is an A.

There is, of course, no reason to think that this is the only inference form which exemplifies the generation of post-systematic claims of the relevant sort. Moreover, there is no reason to assume that the logical form of rules of interpretation can be specified more precisely than indicated without taking sides among rival systems. It is, I would say, quite reasonable to suspect that the form to be given to such rules in a system is determined by the nature of the system itself and thus is to be taken as system-relative. The inference indicated (or something like it) goes through on several different interpretations of such rules, e.g., as identities, bridge-laws, correlations, or even as mere imperatives. Part of the outstanding issue involved is the range of the relevant non-systematic terms which are allowed to be covered by the rule. If such terms are only to be those theoretical or technical terms taken from pre-systematically acceptable theories, then the rules have the status of (broadly speaking) "rules of explanation." If such terms may include those from the rough and tumble of everyday life and discourse, the rules conceived are more like what might be called "rules of adequation." In regard to the former but not the latter, the issue of "reduction" is relevant and the reasonableness of the expression of such rules in terms of identities or correlations is enhanced.

My reasons for thinking that "rules of explanation" are, in an important sense, internal to a system, but that so-called "rules of adequation" cannot be, will become transparent later. For the time being, let me only say that rules of interpretation of some sort must be construed as internal to a system, insofar, that is, as that system is considered to be something which may be said to have meaning or significance in regard to any antecedently specified subject-matter. To consider the applicability of a set of systematic statements by themselves, at least as Christian conceives them, i.e., apart from some understanding of what they can "mean" for everyday or pre-systematic affairs, is as vacuous as attempting to classify all things as x's, y's, and z's without further clarification as to what these letters might range over. This is to say that the important notion of system for the purposes of its assessment in terms of the A-conditions is that of an *interpreted* scheme of notions and principles. It is a consequence of this that the distinction between these two sorts of so-called "post-systematic" statement, namely, rules of interpretation and generated claims, is more revealing of the structure of a system than that between "systematic" and "post-systematic" statements which is drawn in the formal way indicated earlier.

A second and, for our purposes, more important difficulty with Christian's division may be illustrated by an extremely crucial statement which Whitehead makes in *Process and Reality*.

> 'Actual entities' . . . are the final real things of which the world is made up. (*PR* 27)

This looks again like one of Christian's post-systematic statements, for it involves the use of one systematic term, 'actual entity', and others which are non-systematic. But the truth is that this statement serves a function other than either the result of an application of the systematic to the non-systematic or the provision of a rule for making an application. It is, rather, Whitehead's claim to the effect that his categoreal scheme tells the story of what is real, that his system is true of reality, that he is doing ontology. It is what Christian might well have called "meta-systematic." In fact, it is a sort of metasystemic claim of the sort we have termed the R-claim. It links the system as a whole to a certain subject-matter in a certain way.

4. It is time now to be a bit more systematic about the structure of an ontological system. Let me say, then, that such a system is, to use Chris-

tian's language, embedded in a more generous set of claims as indicated below. You will see that the divisions between the systemic and the extrasystemic are drawn functionally rather than in the formal manner as suggested by Christian.

    I. Presystemic claims
   II. Systemic claims and other elements (system = S)
      A. the categoreal scheme (= C)
         (i) categoreal logic(s)
         (ii) categories of entities
         (iii) categoreal principles
      B. rules of explanation (= RE)
      C. integrity provisions (= IP)
  III. Metasystemic claims (linking claims),
        where: R = reality, L = life, and T = theory (the totality of limited
        but "correct" abstract schemes)
      A. an R-claim (= RC)
         e.g., S_1 is true of R
      B. a general applicability claim (= AC)
         e.g., S_1 is applicable to any item of L
      C. a general explanatory claim (= EC)
         e.g., S_1 is explanatory of T
      D. specific applicability and explanatory claims
         e.g., S_1 is applicable to *this* item of L
  IV. Postsystemic claims
   V. Transsystemic claims
      A. standards of adequacy
      B. standards of explanatory success
      C. standards of determining whether any R-claim is true
      D. the basic ontological principle (= BOP)

One may consider this as representing the constituents of a general ontology, from its core, the *categoreal scheme* C, to a *system* S which includes, besides C, RE and IP, to what might be called an *ontology* O (S + RC + AC +EC), to an *extended ontology* EO (O + all claims of specific explanatory success of O, i.e., O expanded by means of RE to include some specific theories in T). Then, the *general ontology* GO which one holds might be said to include everything on the list, from I through V. Surely a work in general ontology must address all of these constituents.

Let me now discuss briefly the constituents of S. I will in due course turn back to a consideration of the metasystemic and transsystemic claims indicated.

A. The Categoreal Scheme

(i) Categoreal Logic(s)

This includes, first of all, the logic which is adopted as the basic logic of C. For example, it may be classical logic, constructivist logic, or some other system.[9] In addition to this basic logic which is to be taken as presupposed and exemplified by the categoreal principles as they apply to the most inclusive divisions of categories, there may be a distinct logic which is specified as applying to less inclusive divisions. But whatever logic or logics are adopted in the categoreal scheme, any further application or employment of that scheme will carry that logic with it; that logic will be the logic for any talk about reality or life which employs systemic terms.

(ii) Categories of Entities

Traditionally, there is offered a most general division of sorts of entities, such that every entity to which reference may be made in the system is of one and only one of them. Alternatively, such a list may be provided within a categoreal principle which indicates an order of priority (of some specified sort) among them.

(iii) Categoreal Principles

A mere collection of categoreal terms and a logic are not enough. There must also be a set of disjunctive, conjunctive, or inferential statements regarding them and the entities which fall under them. Among these there may be principles of the further division of the categories of entities and principles governing their relationships to each other and the more general sorts. All such principles, as well as the formulae of the categoreal logic(s), are S-analytic.

B. Rules of Explanation

These serve as rules of a schematism, linking C with what arises in L as a part of T, i.e., a more limited scheme of concepts and principles. Whatever can be experienced or thought, but cannot be brought within some scheme of intelligible discourse, cannot be brought within the scope of the schematism. (Standards of the adequacy of these rules and of the success of their application in any case fall outside C, indeed outside any particular O or EO.) These rules are all of a sort. They give directions for translating from the language of certain domains of T to the categoreal language of C. In this role, they might better be called "aids to digestion," for they allow an accrual of some domains of T to O by assimilating the language of T to the language of C. This integration of T and O is, in effect, an expansion of O to EO.

C. Integrity Provisions

These are provisions for maintaining the integrity of S in the face of the strains, shocks, and buffetings imposed by L (which latter must remain unspecified in S). They must not be confused with standards for the adequacy, explanatory success, etc. of S or any part of S, for the latter are necessarily external to S. A system may be proposed which contains no such provisions; it is not clear that it must provide any in order to be a genuine ontological system. In any case, they seem to be of two sorts.

(i) Filters

These are devices for insuring applicability of S by ruling out of court the legitimacy claims of certain sorts of presentations or articulations of what appears in life. They may involve the specification of priorities of evidential status or they may simply disallow consideration of anything under a certain manner of description or specification. These are the closest things to rules of adequation to be found in S and are, thus, similar to rules of explanation. However, there can be no rules of adequation in a strict sense, since, apart from reference to some domain of T, i.e., some intelligible scheme of abstractions, no items of L can be identified within S. Filters must not be construed, therefore, as having reference to particular sorts of experience, thought, or whatever which may arise in L, but only to how they may be considered. Analogously, a certain scientific system may include a filter according to which nothing is to be considered unless it can be presented in terms of measurements, even though its avowed subject-matter is not identified merely with a certain domain of measurements. In regard to ontology, one might suggest that such devices build a blindness into S. This is true enough, but it is a color blindness rather than an absence of sight. In any event, it must be allowed that a filtering ontology begs the issue of its adequacy to life to just that extent.

(ii) Amenders

These are provisions for revising the system by either deciding which among certain items in S are to be culled or directing changes in or additions to the items of S. Like the provision for amendment of the Constitution of the United States, this may specify procedures, not only for adding to S, but for changing any item in it, including the amenders themselves. Since the justification for having an amender M for a system S_1 seems to be that of helping to ensure the satisfaction by S_1 of the A-conditions, one may think that M must fall outside S_1 in such a way that a metasystemic claim linking S_1 and M can be made. Perhaps what is thought to be involved is a claim of this sort: S_1 can be made to better conform to A-conditions only as specified by M. This would indeed be a metasystemic claim; it is a metasystemic claim regarding M. But this does not in any way show that M itself is not a part of S_1, which is the point at issue. We should not in any case confuse the amender itself with its application or with any justification which may be offered for its being invoked in the introduction of a change into the system. It is applied from without the system (by the ontologist) in view of considerations made in regard to the satisfaction of A-conditions which also fall outside the system, but if it is a part of a whole which may be assessed in light of the A-conditions, it belongs to that whole. After all, many elaborate systems may include minor inconsistencies or incoherences which we would agree are non-destructive, for we seem to sense that these problems are local or peripheral in view of the priorities or indications "set by the system itself." What we have in mind, it seems, is that something within the system allows its own purification. Of course, one may hold that any altered system is a new system, so that an amender cannot be a preserver of the system to which it belongs but only a device for creating another in which, to the extent that the new system is coherent, the amender itself has been replaced. This issue of what might be called "system identity through change" by and large admits, I think, of decision by convention. In any case, it is, so far as I can see, irrelevant to the issue of whether an ontological system may include an amender.[10]

In saying that the constituents of a system may be exhaustively sorted into one or the other of these slots, I have not addressed the issue of whether a system logically must or should have constituents of each sort. Certainly, not all so-called systems which we may run across in the history of philosophy are so articulated as to allow us to identify all of these parts. Most often, it seems to me, we confront truncated systems in which certain elements are simply absent. Even in the best, for example those of Aristotle and Whitehead, rules of explanation are employed, it would seem, without always being clearly stated, and the formulation of integrity provisions are overlooked entirely. We have to dig such things out of the discussions and arguments and try our hand at postulating their forms. In general there seems to be covertly involved in most purported systems some general notion of the proper "look" of evidence and therefore of what may count for or against the system itself. It seems to me that the main reason one finds it difficult to assess the relative merits of the grander systems and to adjudicate between them is that they tend, in their aim at comprehension, to include such self-enhancing and adaptive principles. I shall return to this point down the road a bit.

5. One important component of the set of categoreal principles, which, it seems, must be present in any coherent system in which there is a plurality of categories of entities, may be singled out for special attention. This is the principle which specifies a dependency or priority among the named sorts of entities of the system so as to provide an asymmetrical reading of whatever constructions, derivations, or explanations may be drawn from or made on the basis of the system. I shall call this "the primacy principle" for short. If a system S is an ontological one, then, the primacy of entities of a certain sort P as specified by a principle of this sort may be said to be, given the satisfaction of certain further conditions, a case of *ontological primacy.*

It can be easily seen that there are two such conditions on the primacy so specified in order that it be characterizable as ontological. The first is that the RC, which provides for the very ontological character of S, be capable of formulation in such a way as to make reference to P. The second is that S be structured in such a way that that reference to P provides for the placement of P within a certain ontologically significant ordering of sorts. According to the first condition, the RC must be able to gain entry to S by way of P. According to the second, that entry must conform to a schema, transsystemically provided and systemically adopted, for the allocation of categoreal sorts into a primary/secondary (or perhaps more complex) division. I shall shortly propose a reading of this schema in terms of what I shall call "the basic ontological principle" (BOP).

Thus, we have three separate principles operating in the simple determination of entities of sort P as ontologically primary, namely, the systemic principle which I have called the primacy principle, the metasystemic reality claim so formulated as to specify P, and the transsystemic schema for ontological ordering among entities by sort. What results from the operation of these three items is a characterization of S as an exemplification of a schema with unique ontological significance; it is a depiction of S as an ontological system by reference to its very structure. (One must never forget, however, that this characterization, which is an alternative to the "S + RC" characterization, presupposes the RC for its explication.)

The above is so abstract as almost to make one cry, but, fortunately, it receives clear illustration in Whitehead's system, which in this respect as well as so many others, is more carefully crafted than most. Consider the following:

The basic ontological principle:
  Anything there is is either
    (1) an ontologically basic entity,
    (2) an aspect of an ontologically basic entity, or
    (3) a plurality of ontologically basic entities.

Whitehead's primacy principle:
  Of all categories of entities that of actual entity is primary.

Whitehead's "specified" reality claim:
  All and only actual entities are ontologically basic entities.

The exemplified basic ontological principle for Whitehead's system:
  Anything there is is either
    (1) an actual entity,
    (2) an aspect of an actual entity, or
    (3) a plurality of actual entities.

Now, we may do the same sort of thing for Aristotle merely by substituting 'primary substance' for 'actual entity'.

One important payoff for all this is that it clearly illustrates the significance of the RC. Without it the categories of entities cannot be said to have ontological import. Another is that it shows how the BOP provides a basic structure to which the categories of entities must conform, thereby providing cohesion for the system as a whole. Nevertheless, both the "specified" RC and the BOP are quite vacuous apart from the further specification of a relevant sense for each of the nonsystemic terms involved, namely, 'anything there is', 'ontologically basic entity', 'aspect', and 'plurality'. Such specification cannot, as we well know, be provided by invoking the categoreal scheme itself, since the terms are, as is the term 'reality', nonsystemic. The specification of these terms is, in fact, one with the unpacking of the term 'reality' in the general RC, which we have already seen to make a reference outside the system. To recur to an earlier way of putting the same point, the term 'reality' in the RC and the phrase 'anything there is' in the BOP refer, collectively and distributively, to the subject-matter of ontology, which must be designated independently of the system. That is, in an investigation guided by the question "What is reality?" there is, logically prior to its phases of theory construction, a designative phase within which these terms must receive a referential precision. The terms 'ontologically basic entity', 'aspect', and 'plurality' (or some such cognate terms) must, then, receive a similar treatment within the same phase. Further consideration of these methodological matters must await the next chapter, wherein the phases of ontological investigation will be discussed more appropriately.

Let me now, in closing this section, pay some passing attention to a certain objection which may arise regarding the above formulation of the BOP. The objection is that it precludes the possibility of a certain sort of ontological system in which more than one of the categories of entities can be specified as being a category of ontologically basic entities. Such a system might be "ecological" in the sense that several categories require each other and are equally basic. Indeed, there may be a perfectly respectable system in which each category of entities provides an ecological niche in an encompassing ecology of niches, so that reference to "aspects" (though clearly not pluralities) is somehow out of the question. I have sympathy with the sort of ecological vision which underlies this objection, but I do not think that it serves to undercut the legitimacy of the BOP. In order to see this, two things about the BOP must be noted.

First of all, the three divisions are indeed intended as both mutually exclusive and exhaustive, but there is no assumption involved that each must be instantiated. It remains true that every thing there is is either an ontologically basic entity, an aspect, or a plurality, even if, according to some ontological system, there is nothing that is that falls into one or both of the latter divisions. An ontological system of absolute idealism (if there can be any such thing) would dispense with pluralities, though not aspects. Certain nominalistic atomisms, whether materialistic or phenomenalistic, might attempt to dispense with aspects but not pluralities.

The second thing to note is that a set of categories of entities in a system may well be drawn without regard to the divisions of the BOP. There is nothing, for example, to preclude a variety of subsorts of ontologically basic entities from being listed in a table of categoreal sorts along with sorts of a more general level. Suppose, for example, that Aristotle had exhaustively divided primary substances (his ontologically basic entities) into men, dogs, and "unmandogs." Then suppose he had contrived a list of fundamental categoreal sorts somewhat as follows: men, dogs, unmandogs, universals, and individual accidents. Mutually exclusive and exhaustive this classification may be, but it is surely unperspicuous. No single one of these five "categories" could be said to constitute the class of ontologically basic entities. In truth, doesn't Aristotle actually do something like this, though in regard to "aspects" instead of ontologically basic entities, in his list of nine nonsubstance "categories?" Whitehead provides a clear case of a sorting of entities which is unperspicuous in regard to the three divisions of the BOP as I have framed it. Of his eight so-called "Categories of Existence," one is eliminable (as falling under another), one specifies the sort of entity which turns out to be ontologically basic, three are clearly something like "aspects," two are clearly pluralities, and another (contrasts) is, depending on one's interpretation of Whitehead, indeterminate as regards the last two divisions. (This is not a criticism of his way of doing it, of course, for there may well be other and even more crucial uses for such a list than this one.)

In any case, the point is now made. The "ecological" objection may be met by one or both of these observations. That the BOP may be somewhat trivialized in the process remains a clear possibility. It is even conceivable, though I cannot quite picture how it would go, that quite *every* thing there is falls into the division of ontologically basic entities and in such a way that the most general sorts of entities are "ecologically" related. Nor can the application of the BOP to such an extreme ecological ontology be said to be vacuous, for even in this case it would serve a crucial ontological function, namely, that of providing a means for saying that every thing there is is neither an aspect nor a plurality, but rather an ontologically basic entity.

6. An ontological system carries with it, by virtue of being ontological, claims to truth, comprehensiveness of application, and explanatory power. It is successful to the degree that it fulfills these claims. But there are conditions which must be satisfied in order that this fulfillment obtain. Whitehead illuminates some of them in a well-known statement.

> Speculative Philosophy is the endeavour to frame a coherent, logical, necessary system of general ideas in terms of which every element of our experience can be interpreted. By this notion of 'interpretation' I mean that everything of which we are conscious, as enjoyed, perceived, willed, or thought, shall have the character of a particular instance of the general scheme. Thus the philosophical scheme should be coherent, logical, and, in respect to its interpretation, applicable and adequate. (*PR* 4)

So far forth, this could be a description of universal science, since no requirement of being true of reality is mentioned in this context. We have just seen how it is that Whitehead inserts the RC into his larger view. In any case, let us see what we do have here.

As Whitehead's subsequent remarks would seem to indicate, an acceptable system must not only be coherent, consistent, applicable, and adequate, but it must both exhibit a logic which allows inference, exemplification, and construction and claim necessity in its comprehensive applicability. The last two points should, I think, be treated as conditions, not of acceptability, but of the defining structure of an ontological system. It is a necessity of the categoreal scheme itself as I have depicted it that it contain a categoreal logic, though whether it need to conform to Whitehead's own view of the proper logic and its powers (which is just the logic of *Principia Mathematica*) will here remain an open question. As to the condition of necessity, I take it that the point is that one or more of the metasystemic claims earlier mentioned be so formulated as to include a necessity operator of a *de re* application. At least this much is true: no linking claim of the system to reality, life, or theory can be formally or analytically true.

Consistency, I take it, is a transsystemic condition upon the system, i.e., its satisfaction is not to be identified with any application of a categoreal logic considered as such. If its satisfaction involves reference to any "logic" at all, that logic would have to be a transsystemically invariant one which can somehow be elicited from reflective reasoning alone and from the employment of that reasoning in philosophical dialogue as it might be shared by philosophers of very different systemic persuasions. The possibility of such a general logic of dialogue should not, of course, be confused with any specific attempt at the articulation or formulation of it, which would itself constitute a theory of it and may well be, for that reason, systemically skewed. Satisfaction of this condition, then, could only be tested dialogically, and it is perhaps not too much to say that the early, Socratic dialogues of Plato provide a model for how this may be done.

The condition of coherence is equally important. It is the requirement of the systemic inter-relevance of the items in the system. This rules out the sort of internal independence of categories and principles which would allow a root dualism or an even more extensive disconnection of things. The important criticism of Descartes' metaphysics is not that it is inconsistent, but that it is incoherent. The main force of the criticism that a certain claim in a system is *ad hoc* is not that it was framed in order to deal specifically with counterexamples, but that in being so framed it introduces an item into the system which is not coherently integrated with the other items. Similarly, the criticism of a system that it is unparsimonious is perhaps most often a criticism, not of the multiplication of entities and principles beyond a certain standard of elegance, but of the fact that such a multiplication introduces a failure of relevance between some of the principles or entities.

On Whitehead's explanation of them, adequacy and applicability are difficult to get straight. Adequacy seems to indicate comprehensive applicability, a condition which is then understood as directed to any and every item of *life*; this is indicated in the AC as formulated above. The "applicability" of the system to the full extent of *reality* seems not to be involved. Let us distinguish two conditions under the temporary titles of "adequacy to life" and "comprehension of reality." What is puzzling, of course, is how the satisfactions of these conditions are to be tested. Neither the items of life nor those of reality can be identified by the system itself, unless we are to conclude, as we should not, that the system is self-validating. This means that there cannot be, in addition to rules of explanation, rules of adequation and comprehension in the system itself. Somehow the system must remain open to disconfirmation from sources which are not theoretically prestructured. The terms 'reality' and 'life' are just the sort to carry this connotation. Adequation may, of course, be understood as the test of seeing how the system survives in the tumble of everyday life and within the fires of philosophical dialogue. But comprehension of reality cannot be so obviously illustrated.

This reference to reality forces us to return to the consideration of the RC and to the notion that there is a subject-matter which ontology claims as its own and of which it purports to speak truly. From this angle we can see that the condition of comprehension of reality is just the necessity that there be a coincidence of the system with the full extent of that subject-matter as designated and that it reflect any general structure which that designation may itself reveal. Indeed, the point of engaging upon the ontological enterprise is just to arrive at a general account of that subject-matter with which it claims designative coincidence. It is important to see this. The ontological enterprise is *not* an endeavor to frame a system which is adequate to life. It is an endeavor to frame a system which is true of reality. It is an assumption, if you will, that a system which answers truly and comprehensively to reality will *also* be adequate to life, since reality at least includes life and since, as I shall argue at a later place, life in its fullness and concreteness provides our only access to reality. So adequacy to life is a legitimate condition upon an ontological system, even though the fulfillment of that condition is not the purpose for which the system was constructed. The difference between universal science and ontology remains radical.

So now we have as A-conditions on an ontological system these:

(i)   consistency
(ii)   coherence

(iii)   adequacy
(iv)   explanatory power
(v)   designative coincidence

The condition of explanatory power was introduced earlier and is taken here as more or less self-explanatory. The condition of designative coincidence is the same as that of "comprehension of reality," but under what I take to be a more illuminating label. To these I now add

(vi)   prerogative fit
(vii)   informative impact

7. The final two are easily understood as conditions, but difficult to grasp as providing means for testing the acceptability of an ontology. Each is worth a moment's attention in its own right.

By the condition of prerogative fit, I mean to indicate the necessity that, *should there be a favored access to reality*, the system should favor a fit to those structures which are disclosed by that means. Fit is not the same as "adequacy to," nor is it quite the same as providing an "explanation of." By adequation, each item of life exemplifies some item in the system. By explanation, each principle of local theory is covered by a principle or set of principles in the system. But there is a fit between the structure of the system and a disclosed structure to the degree that they approach identity. Such a fit to a favored structure, if there is any such, should also be favored, which is not to say that the fit should be rigid or absolute, but that it has priority, given equal adequacy, coincidence, explanatory power, and so on, over that with any other less favored structure. The relevance of this to the *testing* of a proposed system in order to determine its overall acceptability is that, conceivably, alternative systems could be equally satisfying in regard to the other conditions, at least so far as could be reasonably tested, and that, in view of this, fit to the favored provides an additional means for deciding between them. Methodologically speaking, i.e., in respect to the process of *constructing* a system, the concern for prerogative fit is of further importance, since, were favored access available, the aim at prerogative fit would serve to guide the process. One would do well to give priority to such disclosed structures in his speculation. The development of this point, which is central to the thesis of this book, is the primary concern of the next two chapters.

Finally, there is the nebulous notion of informative impact to be accounted for. I take it that a minimal system, one framed in such high generalities that the categories and principles are almost devoid of content and few in number, might easily meet the first six conditions. But it would also seem that the construction of such a system would have little informative value and be of less than consuming philosophical interest. What one hopes for in an ontological system is that, in being true of reality, it also illuminate reality, cast it in a light which allows us better to grasp the workings of things. Of course, there is a relativistic aspect to this. What has informative impact for one person or from one point of view may not for another. But this relativism diminishes, I think, with philosophical sophistication. Or at least it may become less relative to individuals *per se* than to the larger historical contexts of philosophical thought.

This notion of informative impact is fuzzy enough for anyone. One may wish to provide it with greater clarity and to diminish its relativity by recasting it under the condition of adequacy or explanatory power. Stephen C. Pepper, for example, interprets the condition of adequacy as incorporating the two constraints of scope and precision (76). Adequacy demands, he seems to want to say, both breadth and discriminating focus in the applicability of a system. A system may be said to be more or less adequate, then, to the degree that it is more or less precise in its ability to discriminate among the details of life. We might agree with this. But whether an increase in the ability of discrimination provides for an increase in informative impact is another matter. It is not clear to me that it always does. As regards explanatory power, one might wish to incorporate into the notion, not merely the ability of a system to "cover" the principles of a range of local theories, but the ability to provide for the generation of such theories by means of an enrichment of the rules of explanation. Such a manner of increasing explanatory power always, of course, runs the risk of introducing incoherence into the system. In any case, such an expansive system need not, it seems to me, unfailingly provide significant informative impact relative to every context of philosophical interest. We should remember that more information, even more precise information, does not necessarily provide for greater informative illumination. It is not quantity, but something closer to quality that is at issue here.

8. The A-conditions on ontological systems do not provide clear-cut, unambiguous standards for accepting, rejecting, favoring, or disfavoring such systems. One reason for this derives from their transsystemic nature, for they involve notions—consistency, adequacy, life, reality—which lie necessarily outside any theoretical framework which might provide them with a more precise application. Another reason is that the ontologist, in his very concern for comprehension and adequacy, must attempt to assimilate any accepted *formulation* of the A-conditions to his

system, to provide a place for them within his net of adequacy and co-incidence. A formulated standard of adequacy must conform to whatever integrity provisions of the sort which I called filters there may be. Any test of consistency must make its peace with the categoreal logic. Any criteria of explanatory power are at the mercy of the elasticity of the set of principles of explanation. In general, what looks bad for the system from an outside view may look quite good from inside.

The slipperiness of the A-conditions is nowhere more obvious than in regard to the attempt to adjudicate between rival systems. From the standpoint of each such system, it is clear that the others will be worse off. This seems to suggest, then, that one must, in order to adjudicate, take a genuinely neutral standpoint and, thus, a standpoint outside every system. But what standpoint could this be? There seems to be, in the first place, no standpoint which can provide the appropriate surety and clarity other than that which involves the application of a system. Of course, there are standpoints which are not tied to a system, namely, those of practice, the mythic, the religious, the aesthetic, and the reflective. Even historical and scientific consciousness seem, though theoretical, to be devoid of commitment to any ontological system. But again, these lack the kind of concern and discipline which seem required for the critical examinatioin of rival systems of an ontological sort. Indeed, it should be obvious—and this is the second point—that the only standpoint from which one could perform the critical task of such adjudication would be that of philosophical reflection itself. But is there a neutral philosophical stance? Isn't the adoption of that stance always relative to a certain favored set of critical equipment? And isn't it the case that the use of such equipment goes along with, involves the presumption of, a system, however vaguely understood?

Everett W. Hall worried this problem almost to death in his remarkable book *Philosophical Systems*. Towards the end of his discussion of various unsuccessful attempts at adjudication, he makes these comments.

> It will be remembered that we left off with various rival philo-sophical systems each claiming to make meaningful and in some sense true, but not empirical, statements about some extra-philosophical world. Yet each, in its dispute with the others, judged the issues in debate from its standpoint and used its cate-gories to set them up. The world does not appear in its own right to decide this contest. One can get at the common object here only through the various rival characterizations of it. What to do? A sheer relativism that simply says, "Be happy with any philosophy which, by some chance, you have got yourself involved in, for

there is no rational choice between them," will not do. This indeed is one of the contestants and should not be favored without reason above others. So we are faced with the problem of trying to get out of our categorio-centric predicament and coming to terms with the universe by means of something given to all philosophical constructions. (127–28)

Hall's concluding chapter, which investigates the possibility of finding a given by appeal to which adjudication can be brought off, is not promising. The upshot of his own view is indicated by the very last paragraph in the book.

The grammar of common sense united with the structure of our natural experience forms, I suggest, the highest court. Beyond it there is no appeal. But its verdicts are not certainly true; it itself challenges them; it does not speak with one voice; and since we are concerned with matters of truth and not merely legal decision, we must acquiesce to the insecurity this finally forces upon us. (164)

Now this conclusion looks like an assent to nontheoretical life in its fullness, including the use of ordinary language, as the basis for adjudication. This hardly seems to improve upon the test for adequacy which we have discussed. Or is it, by virtue of its concern for "structure," an appeal to the test of prerogative fit? In any case, the familiar problem arises here too. How can we take a standpoint in life upon rival systems without at the same time adopting a philosophical point of view? And how can we do the latter without taking our stand in a system and thereby begging the question?

This difficulty, which seems at first insurmountable, derives, it seems to me, from two oversights. One has to do with what life offers us and the other has to do with what philosophical reflection buys into. Neither is quite as categoreally commissive as might at first appear.

When one looks to life for arbitration, he seems to find either a systematically prearticulated array of evidence or a mere confusion of ambiguous happenings. Viewed in the first light, a system is already at work. Viewed in the second, nothing can be articulated and no clear structure can be elicited until a system is brought into play. But things are not so bad as all that. There are the various stances to be considered, each of which offers a presystemic *structuring* of things. For example, within the practical stance considered apart from theoretical or systemic intrusion and accrual, things appear with a practical ordering, in a terrain, and as having a sort of recognizable fittingness or unfittingness. They appear as anything but a confused panorama of tumbles and tangles. Of course, the purification of the practical stance (or any other stance), the bracketing out of commitments to and biases in favor of this or that system or theory, is a difficult if not impossible chore. But the point is that an appeal to life for the purpose of adjudication between systems is, however often frustrating, not altogether hopeless. Hall's appeal to the structure of ordinary language, if understood as possibly differently disclosed relative to different stances, may be thought to aid in this process.

But still the standpoint of adjudication must, whatever it appeals to as a prestructured given, be a philosophical one. It is incorrigibly critical and reflective. Yet, what is involved is not individualistic; it does not encourage the lone philosopher, feet planted in his own soil, to go things alone. Philosophy is essentially dialogic. The philosophical standpoint which is taken *in dialogue* is at bottom rooted, not in one doctrine or system, but in several. Or rather, it is not "rooted" at all, but by virtue of an appreciation of alternatives, methodologically free to move among them. (The notion of a purely abstract philosophical standpoint, divorced from any consideration of doctrine or commitment, seems to me to be quite ludicrous.) Genuine dialogue is of course as difficult as it is rare. One must be able to take the point of view of the other in order to engage upon it. Is it possible? I think so. To the extent that it is, a sort of neutrality to system is also possible. But it is won only fleetingly I am afraid, always diminished and often demolished by the intrusion of conviction and the comfort it brings along with it.

3

The Ontological Enterprise

♦♦♦   1. Having considered the nature of and conditions on an ontological system in some detail, we may now turn our attention to that form of theoretical investigation which is directed to the construction of such a system. I shall eventually narrow the discussion to a consideration of one of its first steps. It would seem to be desirable, however, to attempt a general familiarity with the full course of this manner of investigation first.

Any theoretical investigation moves through a number of stages, but throughout the course of its progress it persists in carrying forward a certain question which it is the purpose of the investigation to answer. It may or may not be the case that the questions asked in different investigations have the same form. I propose, in any case, to consider only those investigations which raise questions of the same form as that which is raised in ontology, namely, those of the "what is _____?" form. In regard to such investigations two general features should be observed at the beginning. The first is that the "what is _____?" question serves a logically different role at each functionally distinct stage of the investigation. The second is that there is a certain logical order to these stages, though sometimes an investigation may well proceed more fruitfully by ignoring, at least to some extent, the logical order in favor of moving on all fronts at once.

On what I shall call "the standard model" for theoretical investigations of this sort, the stages would seem to be as follows:

(1) *designation*: identifying or locating a limited subject-matter for investigation

(2) *survey*: characterizing that subject-matter in a general way and in terms which are not borrowed from a later stage of investigation

(3) *account*: providing a schema or framework which is interpreted as applicable to the limited subject-matter

(4) *application*: providing an application of the account to the results of completed and ongoing survey

(5) *explanation*: providing, in terms of a background theory or picture, an understanding of why the account holds of the limited subject-matter

(6) *reapplication*: providing an application of the explanation to the results of completed and ongoing survey

It may be seen that, logically speaking, the full satisfaction of the aim of each succeeding stage presupposes the satisfaction of the prior one. One can survey the subject-matter with full confidence only if he has reason to think that he knows what that subject-matter is, that he can demarcate and identify it. One can provide a reasoned account of the subject-matter only if he has that sort of familiarity with it which extensive survey provides. And so on.

It can also be seen that the results of each stage can be taken to provide an appropriate yet only partial answer to the "what is _____?" question or, to put it otherwise, to provide a completely adequate answer to that "sense" of the question which is relevant at that stage. It isn't that the question is ambiguous. It is rather that it has a "phased" complexity of application.

These six stages can be divided into two more general ones. Since the stage of account and the three which follow it have to do with the presentation or assumption of some sort of theory, they may be said to comprise the *theoretic* phase. We may then speak of the first two stages as the *pretheoretic*. Such theoretic and pretheoretic phases are, therefore, equally phases of a *theoretical* investigation. They must, then, be distinguished from what we have had occasion to refer to as "theoretical" and "pretheoretical" enterprises, stances, or activities. I hope the reader will not be confused by this. I will attempt to abide by the terminology involved and, in fact, have already used terms in this way in the previous chapter.

2. Given this, when we turn specifically to the ontological enterprise we are struck by what appears to be a rather discouraging fact. This standard model appears to fit it only with some difficulty. Barriers—which seem to be quite steep, if not insurmountable—to the carrying forward of the investigation in this way appear at each investigative level.

Consider, first, the problem of the designation of the subject-matter of ontology. The term 'reality' is as close to an "official" name for this as we can find, and it is for this reason that I have adopted it. Philosophers today appear to favor it over such terms as 'existence', 'actuality', or 'being', often saving the latter for dimensions of reality at large. But however comforting it may be to invoke a term which has the stamp of common philosophical use, this of itself does not guarantee that such a use is referentially in order or above suspicion. The role of designation is, therefore, not just that of coming up with a comfortable or familiar or intuitively appropriate label, but that of indicating in a clear and generally acceptable manner that the concept or notion of a subject-matter which it is used to elicit is that of a subject-matter which is both genuine and proper to an enterprise which deserves to be called ontological. More specifically, the proposal that the label 'reality' apply to this subject-matter must be spelled out, explicated, in a way which (i) allows one to identify or locate a specific subject-matter, (ii) can be made intelligible and meaningful to contending ontologists, (iii) is open to critical appraisal in philosophical dialogue in regard to its appropriateness for the purpose it is designed to fulfill, and (iv) is independent of and neutral to one's favored categories or ontological system. If the explication fails of (i), it cannot be designative in nature. If it fails of (ii), one can never have any confidence that apparently differing philosophers are really agreeing or disagreeing about the same thing. If it fails of (iii), it closes the door to philosophical consideration altogether. If it fails of (iv), the ontologist has no defense against the accusation that his systemic claims beg the ontological question. This latter point is crucial and calls for some expansion.

Consider the linking claim, the R-claim, which is made of each ontological system. The general form of the claim,

_____is true of reality,

must be such that rival ontologists can employ it equally, can argue for or against the filling of the blank by a reference to one or the other of their ontological systems. It cannot be allowed that any specific claim of this form is true or acceptable merely by virtue of the meanings of the terms involved, as it would be were 'reality' defined as what is delimited in some fashion by the system referred to. The upshot is this. The sense of the general form of an R-claim must be neutral to any reference to a specific ontological category. What is needed is some determination of what the term 'reality' "means" in an investigatively available but pretheoretic sense. It is also necessary to arrive at the operative sense of 'true of'. (The situation is of course similar in regard to other linking or metasystemic claims, i.e., the senses of 'applicable to', 'life', 'explanatory of', 'coherent', and so on require pretheoretic, if not designative, clarification.) Moreover, the BOP, insofar as it is taken to be a transsystemic assumption of ontology, needs explication as well. This is due to the fact that the phrase 'anything there is', as well as the references to ontologically basic entities, aspects, and pluralities, posits the conceivability of a division within reality. Full designation of reality, then, involves the pretheoretic explication of a number of terms which appear extrasystemically yet necessarily in the ontological enterprise. Such terms, as well as many others, may be called "cartographical" in a sense to be introduced in the next chapter.

How are such terms to be explicated so as to satisfy the various indicated conditions? Some might say that what is required is the provision of stipulative definitions, but this is clearly wrong. The concern of ontologists with reality is something they hold in common, so long, that is, as they are genuine ontologists. That this shared concern is the same as that which is determined by a stipulative definition of 'reality' and the other terms can only be decided by explicating the senses of those words which determine the shared concern. Thus stipulation gets us nowhere. Others might suggest that the issue is to be settled by linguistic analysis, by the determination of the use of the relevant words in ordinary discourse. But this won't do either. Words are used variously, 'reality' being a prime example of promiscuous application and homonymy, and it is only a certain use which is at issue. It is in fact not a word but a concept or, if you wish, a notion which is at issue. What is involved, then, is not properly called linguistic analysis but conceptual analysis. Even were there no word in ordinary discourse which, given a certain use, might serve to indicate the subject-matter of the ontological enterprise, we would find it useful to invent one, for, if the ontological enterprise is a genuine enterprise, the concept or notion of such a subject-matter is a shared one. I do not think things are as drastic as that, however, for I think that certain terms of ordinary discourse, sharpened no doubt within the history of philosophy, are available to us to do the job at hand. I believe, therefore—though this assumption may be questioned—that linguistic analysis, performed with an eye to a sense for the concepts involved and their requisite roles in the ontological enterprise, can be a helpful handmaiden to the task of the sort of conceptual analysis which is needed.

But given all of this, there remains the special problem of how properly to carry forward an analysis of the concept of reality. For, unfortunately, the procedure involved in a limited theoretical investigation, i.e., an investigation on the standard model, will not work. In a limited investigation the subject-matter is referentially fixed by indicating certain limits within a larger and already accepted context and thus by identifying the limited subject-matter as that which is to be found within those limits. But, clearly, in regard to the subject-matter of ontology no such context and no such limits are available. That subject-matter is understood from the start to be comprehensive, to be such that its limits are identifiable by reference, not to something which lies outside it, but to what is found within it. Obviously, to indicate that what lies outside it is the "not real" is to presuppose the applicability of the term 'real'. What is needed, then, if ontological designation is to succeed, is something other than the standard and contextual sort of analysis. But what could it be? The issue is critical. If nothing can be found to do the trick, then any claim of the legitimacy of ontology, at least as a philosophically shareable enterprise, must remain ungrounded and, in the end, gratuitous.

My only concern at this point in the discussion is to bring out the seriousness of the designative problem in the ontological enterprise. I will make a proposal for its solution in section 6.

3. When we turn to a consideration of the possibility of survey in the ontological investigation, we seem to run into one blind alley after another. The problem is that we don't quite know how to go about looking for a surveyable subject-matter. We want to survey reality, but all we seem to get, no matter which way we turn, is life and what appears within it. Of course, one may propose an identity of life and reality or, more modestly, claim that life is real and hence a part of reality, but even were we to accept one of these claims, we would certainly have departed significantly from the familiarity of the standard model in doing so. On the standard model, survey is made possible by designation itself, so that the designation of the subject-matter, though indeed not specifying how one is to view it, provides us with a context, a surrounding terrain, from which views might be taken and surveying expeditions launched. Here, instead, we have a process of designating one subject-matter, then identifying another subject-matter, and then making an assumption regarding the relation between the two.

But the standard model aside, even should we accept this move of assuming a relation of identity or inclusion regarding life and reality, we remain in difficulty regarding the manner of proceeding upon the survey. How are we, for the purposes of ontology, to draw any firm conclusions about life? Nothing, it seems, gives one a clue as to how to read it, i.e., how to determine whether the traits he fastens upon disclose the way life really is or the way he is misled to think it is. One is supposed to be surveying life, not in its role as providing a range of appearances, but in its role of being real. And how is one to proceed with that? For universal science the survey of life in its role of appearing is quite enough, for life so understood is precisely its subject-matter. But a survey of this sort does not hit the mark for the ontologist, even on the stronger assumption of identity.

There is another difficulty. How is the assumption of identity or the more modest assumption of inclusion to be understood, as part of the system or as an extrasystemic appendage to the system?

Clearly, were one, within his ontological system, to identify life with reality, he would be an ontologist only by virtue of a further claim that that system, including that identification, is true of the proper subject-matter of ontology. This is merely to say once more that the systemic use of a notion of "reality" should not be confused with the ontologist's metasystemic use of another notion of "reality" in the R-claim. We should strive to keep these notions apart, perhaps by the device of capitalizing the systemically technical term whenever it appears. (So Hegel, the paradigmatic universal scientist, is interested in Reality, whereas Aristotle and Whitehead, to name two apparent ontologists, are interested in plain old pedestrian reality.)

But if, in view of this, one were to attempt to make the identification of life and reality (or the inclusion of the former in the latter) as an extrasystemic claim, he would confront the problems of how this claim is to be provided with either clarity or credibility. As to clarity, the terms 'life' and 'reality' must be given a specificity of use without appeal to any system. The specificity required is, of course, that of referential informativeness. And this can be provided, as we should by now appreciate, only by means of pretheoretic designations of both life and reality. As to the credibility of the claim, one now needs to make out a case for the two subject-matters, so designated, to be so related. And here the plot thickens. How can a case be made? We cannot see by some sort of direct inspection that they are either exactly the same or sustain a part/whole relationship, for we do not know how to go about "seeing" each as a whole. Failing that, only if they are designated in precisely the same act, it seems, could we have confidence in an identification. And this is clearly not the case. They cannot both be designated in the same breath, so to speak, for then the R-claim would have no function and ontology and universal science would be indistinguishable. So much for the claim to identity. An assumption of inclusion seems to have somewhat better footing. We cannot of course solve the problem by designating life by reference to previously designated reality, i.e., as "that part of reality which . . . ," for, besides being a clearly *ad hoc* move, it leaves us with the task of ensuring an identity between "life" so designated and that which we engage upon from day to day and to which it is the business of an ontological system to be adequate. What *does* seem to be the case is that we want to say that life is real, even though the beliefs and commitments made within it may be quite mistaken, and we feel compelled to say this in such a way that we understand the predicate 'is real' in the same sense as we understand the substantive 'reality'. So we cannot help but buy into the assumption of the inclusion of life in reality. This is loose enough for anyone, but it seems to me to be precisely the basis for our conviction that a system which is true of reality will also be adequate to life. It also provides us with the confidence that only through a consideration of life may we claim any genuine access to reality. But, as already indicated, none of this really helps us along in the task of surveying life in its role of being real. The bare fact that in surveying life as such we are also surveying something which is identical to a part or dimension of reality does not allow us to conclude that the central or generic features of life which we may elicit through survey depict or reveal in some fashion the generic features of reality, either as a whole or in part.

Of course, this barrier to ontological survey may be mitigated should there be, *within our lives*, some access to reality which provides a specifiable, limited, and hence surveyable region or dimension of it. Such a limited role for survey would be limited still more were that access to be only favored over others which might also be found within our lives. Such a truncated and diminished manner of "survey" would hardly deserve the name. In any case, ontological designation itself could not, as on the standard model, supply the credentials for the possibility of such access. They could not be provided through the designation nor, obviously, the survey of reality; nor could they be provided within or through application of an ontological system. They could only be elicited in a study like this, which is concerned with the ontological enterprise as a whole, its overall structure and its viability.

4. Difficulties in understanding how designation and survey might work in the ontological enterprise are not the only ones which arise in attempting to apply the standard model of investigation. The tasks of account and explanation, distinguished on the standard model, seem clearly to collapse into one, namely, the task of providing the ontological system itself. Consequently, the two levels of application also become indistinguishable. This should not be surprising. Every account offered in a more limited investigation stands unexplained, calling for a more general

background view which can provide an understanding of why the account holds of the subject-matter it does. But an ontological system is, by hypothesis, the most general and deepest background theory. Beyond it we may not go. It would seem then that the ontological enterprise is devoted to the provision of a theory which is both an account of reality and an explanation of all other well-founded accounts and explanations. Among other things, this means that the system is not itself subject to explanation by theory. The "explanation" of why an ontological account holds of reality can only be that it holds because it is true of reality, because that is the way of things, but this involves, as one can readily see, the provision of no explanatory theory at all.

I can see only two ways of reinstating a division between account and explanation in an ontological investigation, one which, it seems to me, will not work, and one which, on a certain interpretation of an *ideal* investigation, has some merit. The one which fails proposes that the account be identified with only a part of the system, perhaps the categoreal scheme, and that the explanation be identified with either another part of the system or the system as a whole. This will not work because the explanatory part or whole, in order to be explanatory, must provide an understanding of why the account holds of its subject-matter, reality. But this would be to explain why an R-claim holds, i.e., to explain why a metasystemic claim is true, and therefore it would involve an appeal beyond the proposed explanatory part of the system itself. It follows from this, then, that an ontological system cannot explain itself. Please note that this incapacity is distinct from the presumed capacity of a system for the achievement of coherence or systematic interrelevance. Our understanding of *what is claimed* in any part of the system is to be, according to the A-condition of coherence, partially dependent upon our understanding of what is claimed in another part of it, but this is not to say that any part provides an understanding of *why* another part holds of reality.

Another possible way of bringing back the account/explanation division within an ontological investigation is to conceive of that investigation as ideally inclusive of an aim at universal science. By this reinterpretation, one also reinstates a certain role for survey. On this view a system of universal science is proposed as an account of life, which latter is, logically speaking, both designatable and surveyable prior to the construction of the account. Given such a comprehensive account of life, the question then arises: why does it hold of life? To this the only reasonable sort of answer would seem to be that it is necessitated by the way things are in reality. That the account holds of life can be explained, so the proposal goes, only by a picture of the nature of reality.

This enlarged view of how the ontological enterprise ought to work, whereby the project of universal science is taken to be internal to it, confronts two difficulties. The first is that it is not true to the actual history of ontological investigation. This may be how it ought to work, but it is not how it has been most commonly thought to work. Indeed, the project of universal science is, I would say, a relatively recent innovation, largely following upon Kant and those who subsequently took the transcendental turn seriously. But this is not a telling criticism, for one could well argue that earlier ontologists were still struggling with the proper analysis of their problem and that those ontologists who subsequently disavowed universal science as a relevant task simply revealed their continuing insensitivity to the true dimensions of the problem.

The second difficulty is more serious. It rests upon the observation that in the enlarged view of the enterprise there still remains, incorrigibly, two subject-matters, life and reality, and that the last of these has not been given its designative due. In fact, the enlarged view encompasses two distinguishable strands of investigation, one which moves from the designation of life, through survey, to account, and another which moves from the designation of reality, possibly through a sort of diminished form of survey, to explanation. The point then can be made that the second of these comprises ontological investigation in the sense which has been of concern throughout our discussion, even if the two strands together, interwoven and mutually supporting, comprise an enterprise which might be labeled "ontological" in a larger sense. The merit which lies with the consideration of this larger sense is methodological. It may well be that success in the construction of a broadly adequate and widely explanatory ontological system is better facilitated by attention to the demands upon the provision of a comprehensive account of life. I am inclined to think that there is something to this, though I am quite assured that the task of constructing an ontological system cannot wait upon the completion of a universal science. Methodologically, our best hope for success lies in our proceeding on all fronts at once. In any case, I shall confine my subsequent discussion to the structure of ontological investigation in the narrower sense.

We come down, therefore, to a characterization of ontological investigation as consisting necessarily of at least three phases. There is designation, the construction of a system, and its application to life, including the more local theories which are independently acceptable within it. Is there another phase which may substitute for full-fledged survey, namely, the discovery and utilization of limited access? The possibility exists. My argument that there is, though surely discernible by now, remains to be articulated. It awaits further clearing of the ground to which the remainder of this chapter and the next are addressed.

5. Consider now, if you will, that the ontological enterprise consists of a set of activities in which certain philosophers engage. At the level of designation such activities are those of attempting to frame an acceptable set of designative conditions without appeal to systemic claims or terms. At the level of theory they consist of whatever is involved in constructing a system. At the level of application they consist of applying the general to the more specific. Now the question may be raised: how is the work of designative analysis, construction, and application to be carried on so that there is some promise of success?

It may help to note that there is a clear division of talents involved in these three sorts of activities. Those who have a talent for the sort of analysis involved in designation are very often, it seems to me, constructively obtuse. If, as I want to say in a moment, the main ingredient of constructive work is speculation, then the point may be put like this: analytic minds are not always speculative minds. The same may be said of application. Those gifted with constructive abilities are often impatient of application, wishing to leave such "dirty work" to others less gifted. But one may, it seems to me, have a certain critical talent, have an eye for example and counterexample or for formal elaboration, and this is not to be demeaned. There are those who have taken general theories which they did not author and pushed them into areas of applicability which their authors never envisaged. One might also say, in passing, that there are those of great ability in regard to survey, geniuses of phenomenological sensitivity, so to speak, and that this ability is quite distinct from the analytic, the speculative or constructive, and the interpretive, though it perhaps overlaps to some extent with the latter.

We may pause now in order to get our bearings. I have said repeatedly that my concern in this book is with the issue of how best to do ontology. I have also said that my focus in this regard will be, generally, the issue of access and, specifically, the consideration of the possibility of favored access. Slowly, inexorably, we have been moving towards concentration upon that focus. We are now at a point where we can narrow our concentration to the earlier phases of an ontological investigation. Let us put aside consideration of the phase of application and any other activity of testing or tinkering with a system which is more or less fully formed. Though it may be impractical in the long run to attempt to "do" ontology by proceeding in a merely linear way, moving, that is, to the subsequent phases of investigation only after fully and satisfactorily accomplishing the task of the logically prior phases, one cannot expect to proceed with any confidence without attending to the earlier phases in some detail. Proceeding on all fronts at once may in fact be best, so long as this is taken to involve genuine attention to the pretheoretic as well as to the theoretic. Our attention now falls upon those pretheoretic activities, from designating to the doors of constructing. I shall begin the discussion by considering each of these two sorts of activities in turn, but my concern for the possible role of favored access in the construction of a system will lead me to consider what might, methodologically speaking, fall between them, as postdesignative but preconstructive.

6. I come back now to the problem of designation and my proposal for solving it.

The sort of conceptual analysis which is involved in the designation of reality as the subject-matter of ontology must be, as I have indicated, pretheoretic and ontologically extrasystemic. For this, however, it is not enough to consider the domain of everyday affairs and to elicit, by reflection upon it, the conceptual matrix in which a concept of reality (or existence, being, "anything there is," etc.) is shown to be involved. What we may achieve by bringing to reflective explicitness the "logic" of our day-to-day references and assumptions and, assuming its contribution to this, the semantic structure of our "natural" language is important enough, but apart from some manner of grounding or anchoring a reference to reality in some experientially shared and irreplaceable dimension of our lives, such a "logic" must remain merely formal and therefore lacking in any clear relevance to the ontologist's claim to be engaged in an investigation of a genuine subject-matter. The eliciting of a conceptual matrix, that is, would only show that such a term as 'reality' has some use, some conceptual role to play; it would not of itself show that that term or its concept has some application. Thus, the specification of an *experienced application*, as I shall call it for short, is needed.

It should be said in passing that such an experienced application would serve to ensure the significance, not just of a single concept, but of that conceptual matrix in which it occupies a place and serves a specific role. On the other hand, though an experienced application for one concept may provide for the significance of its matrix, only the place of that concept in the matrix can provide for its meaningful employment in judgment, inference, or other discourse. To expand upon a metaphor from Kant, experienced application alone is blind and without discursive meaning, whereas a conceptual matrix alone is empty and without significance. This suggests that, in fact, it is misleading to speak as though a single, isolated concept can be given an experienced application, for it is a concept and the concept it is only in and among other concepts with which it is conceptually related. I think this is correct.

This conclusion, namely, that the cause of ontological designation can be served only by the provision of both a conceptual matrix which includes the concept of reality and an experienced application of that concept of reality, may be questioned. It may be argued that all that is required in addition to that matrix is the experienced application of at least one of its conceptual constituents and that that constituent need not be of reality as such. This makes sense, so long, that is, as an application is thereby allowed for the concept of reality and that application is one which is appropriate to ontological interest. But I do not think we need get at an application of the concept of reality in this roundabout way. As I shall suggest in a moment, we can identify an experienced application of the concept of reality more directly.

Let me consider first, however, the task of eliciting an appropriate conceptual matrix. It seems reasonable to assume that its eventual ontological significance will depend upon certain central terms or concepts which are such as to serve a merely referential use. Terms of a descriptive or characterizing use will, as I have already urged, surely beg the question of the systemic characterization of reality. We may, then, find it helpful to focus our attention on the referential dimension of judgments or claims which are made, considered, or questioned at the "natural" or everyday level. It is difficult to do this without bringing to bear upon our linguistic formulations of such judgments some manner of systemic regimentation,[11] but we can, I think, elicit, without systemic commitment, a very general and purely formal role for the concept of reality. We can employ the term 'reality' in its metasystemic sense to mark out the totality of the referents of the references included in the totality of judgments or claims which we might make. This is, to say the least, uninformative as it stands, that is, apart from some clarification of the referent/reference distinction, some manner of determining references in judgments, and the relevant sense of 'judgments we might make'. But it does provide a basis, by means of a consideration of the diverse and irreducible varieties of reference, for distinguishing and relating such ontologically important notions as those of an ontologically basic entity, a basic sort, an aspect, a multiplicity, and being true of. I will not pursue this sort of formal analysis here.[12]

The identification of an experienced application of the concept of reality must satisfy us on two counts. We must be able to elicit it from a pretheoretical and extrasystemic dimension of our lives which is familiar to and shared by all prospective ontologists. And it must exhibit a reference to exactly the same subject-matter which provides the ground for that distinctive questioning which is ontological. Given these considerations and the discussion in the first chapter, it will hardly be surprising what I shall propose. The reality-claim of practical stancing, considered of itself, satisfies the first requirement, for that claim is a lived assumption of a stance which is both familiar and unavoidable in the lives of all philosophers, whether they claim to be ontologists or not. As to the second requirement, we only need note that the basis of ontological interest and questioning derives, at least as I have argued, from the experienced variety of stances and the diverse reality-claims which can be elicited by reflection upon them. Thus, the experienced application of the concept of reality rests upon precisely the same basis as does the genuineness of ontological interest and the meaningfulness of ontological questioning. In addition to recognition of this fact, all that remains for the proper fulfillment of the designative requirement of ontological investigation is the eliciting of an embodying and role-providing matrix of concepts (no easy task of course) upon which the ontologist may rely in the constructing of a system.

7. Now let us consider construction. Its work is largely speculative, but the field of vision is large and the manner of things which must be kept in mind is varied. There are, of course, no rules for system construction which, if followed, ensure success. Designation, ideally neutral to theory and shareable by diverse ontologists, does not determine or even guide the shape a system may take. From the results of a survey, were it possible of reality, one could not infer the content of that system which would best comprehend and be adequate to it. On the other hand, it hardly seems likely that one could construct a decent system additively, i.e., by the simple process of selecting parts separately and without consideration of the others, for the demands of consistency and coherence are too easily disregarded by such a procedure. It would seem, on the contrary, that an ontological system must be fashioned incrementally in such a way that each increment reshapes the whole and such that, at each such incremental reshaping, the whole may be critically reviewed in regard to its promise of satisfying the A-conditions. The work of speculation must be critically incremental in this way.

Sheer speculation, without any disciplining guidance, is thus unpromising. The unfettered imagination may be productive of something, but seldom of anything worth fiddling with. And this is even more clearly applicable to that speculative activity which is directed to the construction of such a finely tuned machine as a comprehensive system. Thus, if the ontological enterprise is to be considered as responsible, as viable, it would seem that some means of guiding and limiting the speculative imagination must be introduced into the investigative process prior to full-fledged engagement upon the task of construction. Such means must, that is, become fully available at a pretheoretic level of investigation, find its justification there, and, in addition, be of a form which is allowable by the very presuppositions, structure, or aim of the ontological enterprise itself. Let us call such pretheoretic- and enterprise-authorized manners of disciplining the speculative construction of a system *speculative controls.* What sorts of such controls are available?

We may distinguish between two possible sorts, both of which are desirable. The first sort I shall call *limiting controls,* for they function, not to nudge the course of construction along a certain path or in a certain direction in respect to specific content, but to set limits upon the shape of the emerging system. They are authorized, therefore, by the very conditions which, if satisfied, determine the product of construction to be an acceptable ontological system, i.e., those conditions which we have labeled S-, O-, and A-conditions. These conditions on a purported system which has been completed serve, then, to provide controls upon the process of construction itself. Hence, our understanding of what counts as a genuine system informs our attempts to fashion one. Similarly, our concern to achieve a system about which we are willing to make an R-claim provides a sort of check, vague to be sure, in regard to our incremental activity. Of course, whatever limiting controls may be authorized by S- and O-conditions may be so nebulous as to be of little or no disciplining value. In this regard, however, the A-conditions, or at least some of them, would seem to promise more help. Thus, one is precluded from introducing inconsistencies and incoherences into his system, so that one must always check, incrementally, upon the entire system-in-progress in order to detect such structural strains. One must also keep an eye upon interpretive range, upon the incipient explanatory power and adequacy which is involved with each incremental proposal. In addition, one must, if he aims at philosophical illumination, keep in mind the consideration of informative impact. In this regard, a familiarity with the history of philosophy and the problems which have arisen within it is essential.

The two remaining conditions of acceptability on an ontological system, designative coincidence and prerogative fit, deserve a closer look. May they also serve as controls?

Clearly, the bare designation of reality as the proper subject-matter of ontology cannot provide any limits upon the allowable content of the system to be constructed. Of course, the bare designation of reality may not be all of the work that is done at the designative level. If the BOP is assumed, then the explication of its references is a designative business as well and, to the extent that the principle is thus made intelligible, it provides a general structure for the categoreal scheme and thus another control upon the form of the system. We might say, then, that to that extent the aim at designative coincidence provides a limiting control upon speculation.

The condition of prerogative fit offers another possibility. As authorizing a limiting control, it can be assimilated to that of interpretive range, though in a manner somewhat unlike the conditions of adequacy and explanatory power and a bit weaker than either. It is weaker because, though it makes perfectly good sense to say that the greater the degree of adequacy or explanatory power the greater the degree of acceptability, it makes no sense to say the same of fit. A system which has great adequacy but minimal fit is certainly to be preferred to one which has maximal fit but significant inadequacy. To put the matter another way, the degree and manner of adequacy, for example, determines the degree and manner of fit which is significant, but never the reverse. (Note that a high degree of either consistency, coherence, adequacy, explanatory power, designative coincidence, or even informative impact does not in any way regulate the importance of the others.) In sum, considered as authorizing a limiting control, the condition of prerogative fit cannot provide a determination of the degree or manner of fit which is to be taken as limiting. On the other hand, considered as a device for determining the direction of construction or for helping to shape the content of a system, the condition of prerogative fit would seem to provide something a bit more useful. We need to consider the possibility of such a more useful role in more detail.

I turn, then, to a second sort of speculative control which may be called *directive*. Rather than providing a limit upon the accruing product of construction, the system, a directive control would encourage the growth of the system along a certain substantive line. Now it would seem that there are two ways such a control might do this, either (i) by emphasizing certain crucial presystemic truths which must be kept in mind throughout construction or (ii) by authorizing a priority for the inclusion in the system of a fit to a certain presystemic complex of terms in determinate relation. The first of these forms of directive control may be called an *alert*; the second may be called a *cue*. Let me discuss them in turn.

8. As to alerts, they may consist of the results of what Whitehead has called "assemblage."

> . . . before the work of systematization commences, there is a previous task—a very necessary task if we are to avoid the narrowness inherent in all finite systems . . . Philosophy can exclude nothing. Thus it should never start from systematization. Its primary stage can be termed 'assemblage'.

> Such a process is, of course, unending. All that can be achieved is the emphasis on a few large-scale notions, together with attention to the variety of other ideas which arise in the display of those chosen for primary emphasis. Systematic philosophy is a subject of study for specialists. On the other hand, the philosophic process of assemblage should have received some attention from every educated mind, in its escape from its own specialism. (*MT* 2–3)

What Whitehead has in mind is already familiar to us in the list of "presystematic" statements provided in the earlier passage from Christian. Now we can see that this list, rather than representing the results of a survey of a subject-matter, alerts the system-builder to certain avowed presystemic truths about reality which are held to be important, striking, and worth keeping in full view. Not only must a completed system be adequate to them, the system should be constructed with them in mind. One must start with them. They are, if you wish, presystemic assumptions about reality. Yet there is no indication in Whitehead that they must be embodied in or somehow translated into the system. In fact, he tells us nothing about what to do with them except to assemble them and, I suppose, pay them the courtesy of some attention before setting out upon the systematic path. This is well. Their credentials must remain suspect, unless one, as Whitehead does not, takes them to be self-evident or somehow gleaned through a special route of access to reality. How they are to guide us, then, cannot be made more definite. They provide no governing discipline for the growth of a system.

We may now recall that the sorts of speculative controls which we are looking for are not merely to be pretheoretic, but also enterprise-authorized, i.e., they are to be of a sort which a proper understanding of the ontological enterprise would allow a legitimate role. But how may alerts be authorized? If such "truths" of assemblage carry any special weight for construction, then it would seem that the ontological enterprise must somehow authorize their use. Let us say that they are authorized as directive controls only if they (i) are formulable in systemically neutral terms, (ii) carry some extrasystemic claim to truth about reality, and (iii) function in the investigation as revealed through a pretheoretic access to reality. To this may be added the characterization which determines them to be alerts rather than cues, namely, that they (iv) are to be kept in mind throughout construction as prerogative for adequation and hence as signals for the relevance or irrelevance of the incremental growth of the system. There is no notion that the system is to be fitted to them, but only that the system must provide a way of applying to them, of "saving their appearance."

But now, apart from their purported satisfaction of conditions (i) and (iv), how is the satisfaction of (ii) and (iii) by such claims to be made out? More specifically, what sort of claim to truth can be made in their behalf and in what manner may they be taken to result from an access to reality? One wants, that is, some reasonable ground for accepting them as true of reality and the specification of some reasonable way of getting at reality which allows their discovery. And on these matters Whitehead helps us not one jot.

But maybe things are not so bad as they look. If it can be made out that, though life is not the subject-matter of ontology, it is the arena for any access we may have to reality, and if it can be assumed that in the collective hurly-burly of our lives we become sensitized to certain general features of the way things are in reality, then perhaps certain people, ontologically motivated and gifted with a certain abstractive talent, may be able to recognize and formulate the more prominent marks of that sensitization. Moreover, it should not be forgotten that there is a tradition of ontological investigation and a history of dialogue regarding the acceptability of both presystemic and systemic claims. Thus, there is a medium of training in which such a talent for recognition and formulation may be sharpened. In spite of this possibility, it is hard to believe that alerts could ever be very precisely stated or that they could ever be more than tentatively accepted on any particular formulation. Perhaps this is all Whitehead wanted in the first place.

(I have often in the past referred to such crude ontological intuitions as "there are others," "identity across change is possible," and "possibilities exist" as *proto-categories*. That's as good as a name as any. Clearly, on some interpretation they are unexceptionable. But, clearly, on others they are not.)

Interest, then, falls heavily upon the possibility of cues. These, if they existed, would authorize priorities for the construction of a system. A methodological role for the condition of prerogative fit is precisely what would be involved. We may now consider candidates for this role.

9. Is there anything which might legitimately serve as a cue for ontological construction? Let us in considering candidates keep in mind that they must be thoroughly pretheoretic and yet enterprise-authorized. That is, to recur to our discussion of alerts, they must be (i) formulable in systemically neutral terms, (ii) proposed as true of reality, and (iii) authorizable for use in the investigation by virtue of being available through a legitimate pretheoretic access to reality, to which may be added the characterization which distinguishes them from alerts, namely, that they be (iv′) acceptable as carrying a priority for fit with the system. As with alerts, conditions (ii) and (iii) will provide most of our difficulties in

sifting candidates. But before turning to these sorts of difficulties, the notion of fit under (iv') must be made somewhat more intuitively clear. I
shall not try to do much about this here. In the next chapter I will try to
be more specific.

A cue, unlike an alert, calls for its *structural* inclusion, in a certain
sense, in the system, though not in the pretheoretic terms in which it
must be formulated. It calls for such inclusion by being accorded a priority only, for the system which includes it in this way must remain coherent and consistent and must promise adequacy and explanatory power.
All things being equal, the structure provided by a cue must, *in the construction of the system*, be given precedence over contending structures.
To put the matter in a somewhat simplified way, given two structures *a*
and *b* which cannot be equally included in a system-under-construction
at any particular incremental phase of construction, and given that the inclusion of either is equally preserving at that phase of consistency, coherence, adequacy, and explanatory power, then, if *a* is the structure of a
cue and *b* is not, the inclusion of *a* is to be favored over that of *b*. This is
a simplified picture of how things are to be done because the favoring of
a is only to be understood as a favoring of significant similarity to *a* and
not necessarily of its inclusion in toto. The manner of inclusion of a
structure in a system which I have called fit must be understood in terms
of such "significant similarity."

A system which is adequate to some item of experience *x*, let us say,
applies to it by virtue of the fact that *x* is an instance of *y*, namely, one of
the categories, principles, or rules of the system, but such instantiation of
y by *x* is quite distinct from any similarity between *y* and *x per se*. On the
other hand, a system which is explanatory of an "accepted" local theory *t*
does so by providing, by means of rules of explanation *r*, an interpretation of its categoreal scheme *c* which allows *c* to "cover" or perhaps
"generate" *t*, and in this sense it may be said that *t* and *c* are "fitted" to
each other by means of *r* so that a structural similarity between the interpreted or schematized *c* and *t* obtains. Such a "mediated" structural conformity is not what I have in mind by the fit involved in cuing. Any structure disclosed in life can be "fitted" to a categoreal scheme by means of
some rules of interpretation or other. What is at issue in cuing is the "fitting" of a categoreal scheme to a certain pretheoretically disclosed structure by means of the act of modeling the one to the other by direct comparison. Perfect fit would, of course, provide for an identity of structure
at the appropriate level of generality. To favor fit would not, however, be
to promise such perfection. We may let these remarks suffice for the
present.

Now let us consider an obvious sort of candidate for a cue. Let me recall a methodological remark by Whitehead.

> The true method of discovery is like the flight of an aeroplane. It starts from the ground of particular observation; it makes a flight in the thin air of imaginative generalization; and it again lands for renewed observation rendered acute by rational interpretation. (*PR* 7)

I am interested here in the reference to "imaginative generalization." Obviously, it makes a methodological appearance between particular observation and the completed system and concerns the speculative construction of that system. Whitehead elaborates.

> . . . the conditions for the success of imaginative construction must be rigidly adhered to. In the first place, this construction must have its origin in the generalization of particular factors discerned in particular topics of human interest; for example, in physics, or in physiology, or in psychology, or in aesthetics, or in ethical beliefs, or in sociology, or in languages conceived as storehouses of human experience. In this way the prime requisite, that anyhow there shall be some important application, is secured. The success of the imaginative experiment is always to be tested by the applicability of its results beyond the restricted locus from which it originated. In default of such extended application, a generalization started from physics, for example, remains merely an alternative expression of notions applicable to physics. (*PR* 7–8)

Now the relevant point is that such generalization, in order to expand into a system or a part of a system, must involve the preservation of a certain preselected structure but with application to broader fields systemically interpreted. What one expands into systematic application is a proto-system, an order of local things with local relevance. This point is more generously stated by Stephen C. Pepper in his book *World Hypotheses*.

> The method in principle seems to be this: A man desiring to understand the world looks about for a clue to its comprehension. He pitches upon some area of commonsense fact and tries if he cannot understand other areas in terms of this one. This original area becomes then his basic analogy or root metaphor. He describes as best he can the characteristics of this area, or, if you will, discriminates its structure. A list of its structural characteristics becomes his basic concepts of explanation and description. We call them a set of categories. In terms of these categories he proceeds to study all other areas of fact whether uncriticized or

> previously criticized. He undertakes to interpret all facts in terms
> of these categories. As a result of the impact of these other facts
> upon his categories, he may qualify and readjust the categories, so
> that a set of categories commonly changes and develops. Since the
> basic analogy or root metaphor normally (and probably at least in
> part necessarily) arises out of common sense, a great deal of de-
> velopment and refinement of a set of categories is required if they
> are to prove adequate for a hypothesis of unlimited scope. Some
> root metaphors prove more fertile than others . . . (91)

There are differences between Whitehead and Pepper, but both are
looking for a presystemic structure which may be expanded into a system, whether by sheer generalization or analogical extension. Whitehead,
the speculative genius, is willing to consider anything for a start, whether
scientific, linguistic, or aesthetic. It is also clear he feels that the successful ontologist must have some initial feel for things, some comprehensive
insight to begin with. Pepper, the critical philosopher, is struck by the
fact that those systems which come closest to working, which are most
nearly satisfactory in terms of scope, adequacy, and so on, are those
which arise from pretheoretical root metaphors. Moreover, his view is
couched in descriptive rather than normative terms, recounting for us
how philosophers do go about building systems, not how they should
control their speculation. But both philosophers, it seems, have the same
general idea, namely, that the sort of thing which functions as a cue in
the construction of a system is a generalizable or expandable presystemic
structure with obvious local applicability.

There is a great deal of wisdom in these remarks by Whitehead and
Pepper. But their proposal confronts two serious problems, one having
to do with the identification among a range of candidates of a presystemic structure which is to serve as a cue and the other having to do with
the characterization of the range of candidates itself.

As to the first, neither Whitehead nor Pepper have anything to say
about which particular presystemic structures among the available candidates are to be *favored* for fit. Of course, they agree that any favored
structure must fall within the range of those which have some acceptable
manner of application to some area of "common sense fact" or "human
interest," but it would seem that, on their view, any number of such
structures may fulfill that condition of applicability. The problem is that,
methodologically speaking, any structure identified within that range as a
cue must, in the construction of the ontological system, be accorded precedence over other presystemic structures in the range. Any such identified structure must have a normative office in the process of construc-

tion. And this favored status must be presystemically grounded in the fact that it is revealed through a pretheoretic access to reality. Generalization or expansion of a presystemic structure may well be just the ticket for ensuring fit, but only for a properly legitimized structure can a *priority* for fit be authorized. This means that, though a speculator may generalize upon any local structure he thinks might prove illuminating—this being just one of the liberties allowed by the speculative imagination—he cannot give it the status of a genuine cue unless he has good reasons for accepting it, not only as carrying with it a *prima facie* claim to being true of reality, but as derivable by means of some genuinely *favored access* to reality. And neither of these conditions seem to be met by the device of merely taking something one assumes to be applicable at a local level and expanding it towards ontology.

Here something more should be said about the condition upon a cue of derivability through genuine access. Why is it that the proposal of the candidate as true of reality, even the proposal of it as carrying a *prima facie* claim to that effect, is not enough? Why must there be a further condition of access? The answer is that truths about reality may be claimed to be privately arrived at and they may be eccentrically formulated, i.e., in a way which is not available for reformulation by another. Claims to self-evidence or intuitive insight into reality may be of this sort; they will be if a way is not opened which reveals for others as well a region which may be examined. To be genuine, truth may not need to be open to more general scrutiny; verificationists and others of that stripe may doubt this, but they stand, in making that claim, within a systemic context which we cannot presuppose. But access, to be genuine, must be open. It must allow of being shared by anyone who genuinely engages upon the ontological enterprise. The way in must be broad, no matter how narrow the way out.

Now let us turn back to the proposal of the expandability or generalizability of a presystemic structure. This raises the second problem of the determination of what is to fall within the range of acceptable candidates. Whitehead and Pepper both want to allow us to use only such structures as have a strong *prima facie* claim to truth in a limited area. The structures hit upon are thus conceived as initially applicable only locally or partially. There are two infelicities involved in this manner of determining the range of candidates. The first is that the applicability is not specified by them as one made in regard to the appropriate subject-matter, namely, reality. Perhaps for universal science this is not needed, since truth is, in such a case, likely to be truth in regard to some limited area of life. But for ontology this is not enough. Perhaps then we could shore up this deficiency in their accounts by positing a way of access to reality via which we might discover such truths. In regard to this possibility Whitehead and Pepper disappoint us again. For Whitehead it seems any old truth might do. For Pepper there is some restriction, namely, to commonsense fact, but this is not necessarily seen to be an avenue to reality. Nor do we see how it could be. I take it, then, that, by virtue of this difficulty alone, this sort of candidate for a cue fails. As descriptively accurate as it may be of how Whitehead and others may in fact proceed to construct a system, it has no normative force.

The other infelicity in the proposed manner of determining the range of candidates has to do with the fact that each candidate is assumed to be such that, initially and prior to expansion, it is only locally applied. Now this strikes me as an arbitrary limitation. I do not see any justification for excluding from among the range of candidates one which is or is taken to be *already* comprehensive in its scope of application, "world-comprehensive" so to speak. What puts one off from the consideration of such structures could only be, it seems to me, the assumption that any such putatively world-comprehensive structure must already be a system, a product of theoretical construction, and thus the very sort of thing which a cue is not itself supposed to be. But this is a mistake. Moreover, it seems to me that any such putatively comprehensive structure has, by virtue of whatever comprehending success it may have, a *prima facie* claim to favor, just as the degree of adequacy or applicability, even within a limited scope, carries such a *prima facie* claim. To put the point somewhat metaphorically, breadth as well as depth of applicability are considerations of weight in the identification of a cue. And in the context of a manner of comprehensively construing a world, breadth may count for even more. For one must not forget that a claim to truth about reality is a necessary condition on favor and that a structure elicited from a manner of comprehensively construing the world is clearly one for which a *claim* to truth about reality is made in a most obvious and aboveboard way. If a case can be made for a manner of construal of a world as one which provides legitimate access to reality, then the case for a significant depth of applicability of the elicited structure to reality becomes enhanced and the candidacy of that structure for the status of a cue is similarly enhanced. All that remains is the determination of its comparative priority in these regards over other similar candidates. Thus, it seems clear that the limitation in scope of applicability which is proposed by Whitehead and Pepper is mistaken. And from this it follows that the characterization of what goes on in system construction as the generalization or expansion of a structure is misleading. The more generous term 'fit' has been proposed in order to avoid this.

Strictly speaking, the sorts of candidates for a cue proposed by Whitehead and Pepper won't do. Are there any that will, or are we to conclude that legitimate cues are unavailable to the speculator? I have already sufficiently indicated that I believe that there is one candidate worth taking seriously, namely, the revealed structure of the practical arena. The thrust of the second part of this book will be to present such a candidate. The attempt will be made there to formulate it in systemically neutral terms, to indicate its claim to be true of reality, and to indicate the manner of our pretheoretic access to it. But we are not quite yet at a point where that argument can be clearly presented. Such notions as those of access and fit, which I have proposed to employ in behalf of the ontologist, have not yet, I am afraid, received the level of clarity and intuitive grasp which would allow us to apply them with confidence. And since they cannot be clarified for this purpose by appeal to the sorts of "precision" instruments which may be fashioned at the theoretic levels of investigation— being, as they are, already needed at the pretheoretic level—they must, it would seem, not only be gathered from and authorized by the general character of the situation of one's genuine engagement upon the ontological enterprise itself, but be capable of being sharpened for our use by reference to that pretheoretic and, indeed, transsystemic context. In the next chapter I will say what I can about these matters.

10. Let me close this chapter by attempting to recapture, in the terms of the present discussion, the overriding concern of this book.

How is one to begin doing ontology? That has remained our guiding question from the first. It is a methodological question and it requires a methodological answer. We are interested, that is, in what can and what must be done at the pretheoretic levels of ontological investigation. But method must conform to the logical necessities. It is at this point that our troubles begin.

The logical necessities underlying the pretheoretic levels of ontological investigation derive from the fact that the very viability of ontology presupposes the significance of its eventual R-claim, which is to say that an explication of what is claimed when one claims that his system is true of reality must be possible and support for that claim must be shown to be available at least in principle. For the first, one must be able to make sense in systemically neutral terms of the reference made in the R-claim to reality itself. For the second, one must provide some extrasystemic basis or ground for claiming that the system offered is not merely comprehensively applicable to whatever comes to light, whatever may appear in the ambit of one's life, but true of reality as well.

It is the business of the pretheoretic phases of investigation to satisfy these logical requisites. Thus, the methodological aim of these phases is

to anchor the significance of the R-claim of an eventual system in a preliminary way, i.e., so that the investigation can get off on the right foot
and with some decent promise of constructive and interpretive success.
The logical necessity of providing a systemically neutral explication of
the general form of the R-claim is to be satisfied at the phase of designation. There are, as we have seen, difficulties enough about this. But the
logical necessity of providing an extrasystemic and pretheoretic ground
for the application of an R-claim to an eventual system confronts the investigator, not merely with methodological agonies, but with initial confusion as well. To this situation of unease may now be added the exacer-
bation of the special methodological need for the identification at the
postdesignative but preconstructive level of a cue.

The reason for this situation is straightforward. What is needed is a
pretheoretic phase of investigation which satisfies the general aim of survey, i.e., which allows the investigator an access to the subject-matter by
means of which certain general features of that subject-matter may be
proposed. Only by such access to the distinctive subject-matter of ontology can the eventual claim regarding that subject-matter, the R-claim, be
provided with the sort of support which will allow us to construe it as
distinct from the sort of claim which ontology may share with universal
science. But the possibility of survey, at least as performed in any typical
or ordinary manner, seems blocked. Left without guidance from analo-
gous manners of investigation, it is no wonder that the first reaction of
the ontologist, when the difficulty is made clear to him, is a feeling of
confusion, if not, indeed, a sense of deflation and hopelessness.

What is unique to the ontological need for survey lies with two peculi-
arities in regard to its subject-matter. The first is that, as is the case with
life, one cannot get outside of it in order to take a view upon it. The second is that, as is not so clearly the case with life, one cannot, by being
within it, accept *whatever* appears as it appears as being veridically disclosive of its general features or structure. Caught within life and yet unable to accept every position or point of view within it as equally evidential, the ontologist's manner of search for an access to his subject-matter
is set. He can only seek to determine, among the various stances, points
of view, avenues of appearing, manners of consciousness or whatever,
some manner of priority. Indeed, he must seek out the best, for in no
other way may his construction of an ontological system be unambig-
uously guided and his eventual appeal to an R-claim be persuasively
supported.

If ontology is to get off the ground, then, we would have to discover in
our lives, among the ways of viewing things available to us, a favored access, one which could be shown to be more likely than others to be

revelatory of some region which in its disclosed structure accords with the true structure of reality. Such partiality in regard to region and modesty in regard to results would be the best we could hope to come up with as a surrogate for survey standardly understood. But it may be enough to save the viability of the enterprise. If within the confines of our general access to reality, our lives, we could hit upon a favored way of access, then perhaps from that vantage there would be revealed a structure which could serve as a cue to construction, a basis for fit, and thus a ground, insufficient of itself to be sure, for saying that the system is true of reality. At least we could say that the system has *some* clear application to reality. Given that much, we might then have reason to hope that adequacy and explanatory scope carry ontological force.

4

Access to Reality

♦♦♦ 1. When in the course of a theoretical investigation, as this is, a claim is made or a hypothesis entertained, it is wise to attend to the investigative level at which it arises. What is true of claims is also true of the terms which are "technically" employed at any stage. It is important to be clear about the level at which such terms make their initial appearance and receive their imprint of "technicality." Thereby, one can examine the extent to which, if any, the role of that term alters by virtue of its use at other levels.

A technical term is, in the broadest sense, a term employed with a certain instrumental value for the furtherance of investigation, and it may therefore arise at any level, from the designative to the fully explanatory. Often, such terms have a history within the investigation, arising at the lowest presystemic level and then, by passing through successively higher levels, receiving at each a certain shift in application, perhaps towards an ideal of theoretic precision and regimentation. Such terms may be called *protean*. Sometimes, on the other hand, terms which are used technically at a lower level are put aside or replaced with others as investigation proceeds, in accordance with the positing of groupings, identities and differences, and so on which are seen to be more serviceable or illuminating at the higher level. Such technical terms, as indeed all which are "level bound," may be said to be *rigid*. At still other times, a term is fashioned or adopted at a lower level for possible use throughout the course of the investigation. This is certainly the case with regard to those terms which may be employed transsystemically, i.e., in regard to the construction, comparison, and evaluation of theories. Such terms are fashioned at a pretheoretic and systemically neutral level in order to talk about whatever arises in the investigation. This type of technical term I shall call *cartographical.*

The discussion of life, appearing, access, evidence, fit, reality, and so on, to which this chapter is devoted, arises at the pretheoretic levels of designation and survey. Moreover, the terms fashioned for technical use are contrived to serve cartographically. Whether such terms can be gathered protean-fashion into a particular theory is not at issue here. It is only their cartographical employment that is to be considered at this juncture. This is to say, among other things, that no account or explanation of life, appearing, and so on will or should be offered; to do so would be distracting and, indeed, irrelevant to the purpose. It is to say, as well, that the sort of regimentation or precision which we might demand at a theoretic level cannot be hoped for here.

2. Thus cartographically understood, 'life' is proposed as a generic term which collects the plurality of the lives of each of us. Each such life is the life of someone, such that one life goes with one someone from birth to death, and vice versa. There is thus no life without its being the life of someone, and there is no life beyond death or prior to birth. That someone can survive his death would imply, on this technical use of these terms, that his life persists beyond death, which is, given this use, impossible. In so far forth, immortality is not ruled out by this terminology; one may conceivably never die. This is neither here nor there.

What is of further concern is what the lives of each of us are like in their most general surveyable features. A number of things can be said. The life of each of us is the full career of each of us. At a pretheoretic level of consideration, my life is the confluence of whatever I do, think, feel, see, come into contact with, and so on, within the particular circumstances which are present to me as their backgrounds. The relation between me and my life is that I live it. Thus, my life is thoroughly present to me in the sense in which it can be said that I and only I live it. The issues concerning the extent and manner of "consciousness" or "awareness" which is involved in such living presence are most delicious puzzles, but they need not be confronted here, being irrelevant to our present purposes.

What is, however, of crucial importance is a certain dominant trait of that living which does involve awareness, namely, that within my life I am aware of certain things. Specific things come into and go out of my life in such a fashion that I am aware of their coming and going and on occasion their abiding there. They make an appearance in my life and to me in such and such a guise or with such and such features. Their appearing in my life is their appearing to me. They are denizens of my own "stream of life," so to speak.

The term 'appearings' would seem to be ambiguous between that which appears in someone's life and its appearing there. There is the tree perceived and there is the perceiving of the tree. Obviously, we need to be clear about how these cases are to be labeled in subsequent discourse. There seem to be three arguable terminological options. The first is to assume that there are two distinct things involved, one on the side of a subject or perceiver and the other on the side of the object or perceived. This is, however, too harsh a measure, one which introduces an ideal of theoretical regimentation into a unified fact without taking account of that unity. Both the subject/object and the act/content/object distinctions should be avoided at this level. The second option would be to refuse any distinction between the two cases whatsoever, perhaps on the ground that the introduction of a distinction is necessarily theoretical and, moreover, does violence to the unity involved. But this urge to innocence, however well-intentioned, misses the point that in reflective discourse about the facts of life—the very sort of discourse which we are engaged upon now—one thing may be putatively considered in different roles, aspects, or dimensions and from different stances and perspectives within those stances. So, really, the demands of pretheoretic yet reflective discourse are more rigorous and less innocent than the second option allows. The third option shall therefore be adopted. We need three different names, one for the single facts of appearing and two more for the different aspects or cases under consideration. For the first I shall use the term 'appearing'; for the two aspects, whenever it seems appropriate to make a distinction, I shall use 'appearance' or 'what appears' for the one and 'awareness' or 'how it appears' for the other.

The varieties of appearings may be distinguished within my life and apart from theory in regard to both manners of awareness and sorts of appearance. As to the former, one might draw the most general lines of distinction in a number of ways, e.g., as did James in his *Psychology* (245–50), between fringe and focal awareness or, as did Ortega y Gasset in his *Some Lessons in Metaphysics* (48–49), between awareness which is presentative and that which is of the form of "counting on" or, as so many have done, between reflective and prereflective awareness. Or one might, more traditionally perhaps, attempt a sorting into such a variety of manners as seeing, hearing, conceiving, imaging, remembering, wanting, and so on. The delineation among manners of awareness is a matter for sensitive phenomenological survey, but its details may be avoided here, being, again, tangential to our purposes. As to the sorts of appearances themselves, we find again that several different axes of division are possible: "flights and perchings" (James 236), the distinct and the nebulous, the peremptory and the voluntary, and so on. More specifically, the seen, the heard, the believed, the chosen, the said, the feared, the thought, the imaged, the remembered, and all such other things appear to me. The proper categorization of such appearances also falls outside our present concern.

It is important to our purposes to realize that, in the lived confines of my life, what appears is already demarcated and particularized along certain lines. A claim to the effect that what "really" appears in the lives of each of us is a mere qualitative flux is false as it stands. I may, by means of a certain method or regimen, contrive to turn my life into a path such that there is present to me only a flux of appearing, but that turn of events can only be itself something that occurs within my life. In the midst of my life things seldom look like *that*; almost always I am engaged in doing things, moving about, thinking, or whatever, and that which appears in those contexts is already divided, pluralized, ordered in a specific way. There may have been a time in my life when, so the story is told, what appeared was only a big, blooming, buzzing confusion, but my life is hardly like that now. If I must, as I want to maintain, substantiate my theoretic conclusions by appeal to what appears in my life, then I must appeal to it as it appears there. I must begin where I am, in the concrete fullness of everyday life, in my life as I do in fact live it from day to day. *This* is what I am referring to by the term 'my life'.

3. My intent has been to clarify by reference to concrete daily affairs the cartographical function which I wish to assign to the terms 'life', 'my life', 'appearing', 'awareness', and 'appearance'. I wish to provide common coin in terms of which discussion of the ontological enterprise may proceed. We may now move towards a clarification of the notions of access and evidence. For this a closer consideration of appearing and appearance is needed.

To begin, we must distinguish between what appears in my life *as it appears* (appearing *per se*) and my interpretation, depiction, or understanding of it. Of course, my interpretation of what appears may also appear, but if so, it appears as something else, as another appearing. This is not to deny the possibility that at least some appearings in my life involve or contain covert interpretations as they appear. Indeed, it has sometimes been maintained that only on this understanding is the distinction between veridical and nonveridical appearing to be made out. Thus, it has been said that a perception, e.g., my seeing my friend crossing the street, is a combination of a sensory content and an interpretation on it or inference from it and that such perception is veridical only if the interpretation or inference is justified. This is, of course, a *theory* about perception. It holds that perceptions as they appear are interpretive in nature. But note that, as stated, it allows a distinction to be made between a perception *a*, which as it appears is noninterpretive, and the reading of *a* as interpretive, which is or may be another appearing. The wrong move here would be to denominate the sensory content, theoretically posited, as not only appearing but as all that appears. No, what appears when I perceive my friend crossing the street is, as it appears, the appearing to me in a certain manner (i.e., in the manner of perceiving) of my friend crossing the street. Chances are that a sensory content does not appear at all, except as the object of a reference in the appearing of a certain interpretation of the appearing to me of my friend crossing the street.

The distinction which we often make between "seeing" and "seeing as" is drawn, not between appearing as it appears and interpretations of appearing, but between two sorts of appearing *per se*. Suppose I draw a figure on the blackboard, ask you to tell me what you see, and you reply that you see a drawing of a duck. Now suppose I reveal to you that these are just marks on a blackboard which others have reported to be a picture of a rabbit. Then you might say that you can understand this, i.e., how one could see such marks as a picture of a rabbit, but that you, looking again, see such marks as the picture of a duck. There is, I take it, a phenomenological difference in the two cases of what appears to you. In one the appearing is that of a picture of a duck. In the other the appearing is that of some marks on a blackboard as a picture of a duck. The latter appearing as it appears is properly described as a "seeing as," not as a "seeing." Moreover, the appearing which is a "seeing as" is not, *as it appears,* a "seeing" of marks on a blackboard to which an interpretation has been added. A "seeing as" appears as noninterpretive. To say that nonetheless it really is interpretive underneath it all is to invoke a theory.

There are, I now want to say, at least three *dimensions* which an appearing as it appears may exhibit. Let me call them the *datal,* the *significative,* and the *disclosive.* I do not care to argue that these are the only such dimensions (I do not think they are) nor that every appearing necessarily exhibits each of them (I do not think they do). My purpose is merely to introduce a certain pretheoretic terminology which is important to the further development of our discussion.

By referring to the datal dimension of appearing, I mean to indicate the specific *quale* of the appearing as it appears in abstraction from any functioning or tendency which also appears.

By the significative dimension, I wish to indicate a certain range of such functionings which appear. Note that I am not talking about roles, functions, etc., which an appearing may be interpreted to have or which may be, truly or falsely, attributed to it, but only those which it, in its appearing, "gives itself off" as having. This range of "apparent" functionings is that of serving, either in whole or part, as a sign for something. This is vague enough. But it may be exemplified by that variety of signifying which is usually called referring. The point then is that references, referrings, appear in our lives, usually, if not always, together with datal contents (which, by the way, when reinterpreted from the point of view of the references appear as signs). Thus, suppose I perceive Bill's wife crossing the street. The appearing *per se* may, in so far forth, be described as a perceiving of Bill's wife crossing the street. Involved in this is a complex datum together with a number of references. For example, there is a reference in the total appearing to (intention towards) an object which, depending on one's theory of perception, may or may not be said to be a part of the appearing *per se,* namely, the fact of Bill's wife crossing the street. And involved in this reference is also a reference to Bill's wife and another to Bill. These latter two referrings belong to importantly different sorts. Bill is not perceived as present, though reference to him appears with the perceiving which is present. What appears involves reference to both Bill and Bill's wife, but of the two only Bill's wife appears *disclosively.*

This disclosive dimension is not to be confused with the significative or the referential. Bare reference to Bill's wife does not carry with it the apparent disclosure of her in perception. Nor does the addition of the datal component, the bare *quale,* complete the job. Rather, in this example the reference to Bill's wife is not a reference to the datum which appears, *qua* datum, though the appearing may carry with it, as it appears, the character of a "seeing as," i.e., the seeing of the datum as Bill's wife in the flesh. The more likely description would be that my perceiving Bill's wife crossing the street "gives itself off" to be the disclosure of Bill's wife crossing the street. One cannot build up the disclosive dimension of an appearing by lacing together references and data. The disclosive dimension is *sui generis,* just as are the other dimensions.

4. Now the disclosive dimension of appearing is of the greatest importance in what follows. The reason for this is that it is by virtue of its disclosive dimension that an appearing provides *apparent access* to something as it is "really" or "in the flesh." My perceiving Bill's wife crossing the street *discloses* Bill's wife crossing the street and therefore provides apparent (i.e., appearing) access to a certain event or state of affairs, namely, Bill's wife crossing the street, but it remains an open

question whether my perceiving Bill's wife crossing the street provides *genuine access* to the way things really are. As I want to use the term, disclosure may, thus, be (genuinely) accessive or nonaccessive. It may also be general or particular, existential or characteral, direct or indirect. Let me expand a bit on these last three contraries.

What is disclosed may be a particular entity, event, or state of affairs, such as Bill's wife crossing the street, or a general structure or form. Here the distinction of "seeing" and "seeing as" may be helpful. I may perceive a particular event *as* the working of a law or as the application of a type. Whether this is so or not depends upon the appearing as it appears, and nothing else. How the appearing is to be interpreted is another matter. I can see x as exhibiting a general structure y, but conclude that, given my interpretation of x as illustrating a general structure z which is different from y, my so seeing x is illusory. Whether all cases of generic disclosure are in fact cases of "seeing as" is, of course, another question. I shall not pretend to answer it here.

Disclosure is existential or characteral, and perhaps it is usually both. What is disclosed may be the existence of something, say Bill's wife, but it also may be the character, disposition, transformation, or activity of something, say Bill's wife crossing the street. It is sometimes said that the existence of something is always disclosed under a certain description. Thus, my being angry at Bill, insofar as this appears in my life, is said always to disclose Bill as, not merely existing as an object of my anger, but rotten, despicable, ugly, mean, or whatever. This does not seem right to me, but the issue may be put aside as peripheral to the terminological issues at hand.

Finally, disclosure may be direct or indirect. This is to say that what is disclosed may be datally represented in the appearing or it may not. We need to be careful about this distinction. Seeing x as y is not indirect disclosure of x or y, for both are represented in the appearing. Neither is seeing Bill's wife an indirect disclosure of Bill. Bill is not represented datally, true, but neither is his present existence or character disclosed. What is indirectly disclosed must be in any event disclosed. To see how this is possible, consider the appearing to me of a tree. I perceive a tree and that includes the disclosure of a frontside and a backside. But only the frontside is datally present, though this is not to say that it is datally two-dimensional. I perceive the tree as three-dimensional indeed, but only the frontside is datally disclosed. What is indirectly disclosed is the backside of the tree, minimally its character perhaps but fully its existence. And again, though the existence of the backside of the tree is disclosed, that can hardly entail the "true" reality of the backside. An empiricist is wont to say that all indirect disclosures presuppose and, in some decent sense or other, derive from direct disclosures. This seems to me to be wrong on two counts. In the first place, it seems to me to confuse appearing *per se* with an interpretation upon it. In the case of the seeing of the tree, it seems clear to me that what appears as directly disclosed is only a part of what is disclosed in appearing. We do not conclude from first seeing a front side that there must be a backside. What is disclosed is from the beginning something with a backside. How we came to see things in this way, i.e., how we "learned" to have full-bodied appearances like this, is another matter and one of only passing interest to us here. In the second place, it is entirely reasonable to think that there are appearings which are not datal at all but which nonetheless indirectly disclose certain things. Our acts of choosing, for example, seem to me to be of this sort. Indirectly disclosive of an open future, the very existence of the act, and the presence of motivation, they are nonetheless thoroughly nondatal. I have argued for this elsewhere.[13]

A final remark on disclosure seems called for. The cartographical distinction between disclosure and access should not be thought to have anything to do with the theoretic distinction which is sometimes proposed between appearance and reality. The theoretic distinction I have in mind here takes its departure from a certain view of what appears to us in our conscious living, namely, the view that such appearing is distinct from a reality which does not appear and which it is the appearing of. "Appearance," on this use of the term, is therefore a certain stratum of being on its own, a special screen which stands between the conscious subject and that other stratum of being which is "reality." What is involved, then, is a bifurcation of being into two realms. The uses of 'appearance' and 'reality' involved in this distinction are quite different from the uses of 'appearance' and 'reality' as they have arisen in the previous discussion. The latter are not in opposition; no bifurcation is assumed. Nothing in our discussion precludes the possibility that realities are sometimes disclosed in the flesh, that access is sometimes thereby had to the real things. This is another way of saying that disclosure is not on the face of it representational; it does not present itself as standing for something else. Disclosure does not reduce to signification.

5. Thus far I have introduced a host of cartographically technical terms, the most important of which are 'life', 'my life', 'appearing', 'disclosure', and 'access'. We have now to get straight about 'evidence', since it cannot be concluded from a claim that we have access to reality by virtue of the disclosive dimension of a certain range or domain of appearings in our lives—a claim I want to be able to make—that such access provides evidence for favoring one theory of reality over another. Ineffability is not

the only incapacity which has been claimed to come between access to reality and evidence for or against a certain view of reality; the distorting effect of the theoretical stance and the unreliability of memory across dislocative gulfs of experience are other claimants of note.

For someone a to have, within his life, access to something x or, which is the same thing, for x to be accessible to a, x must be disclosed or disclosable through appearing to a. Access, as disclosive, may therefore be general or particular, existential or characteral, direct or indirect, but it may also be broad or narrow, complete or incomplete, informative or uninformative. What is of especial relevance to us is that access to x may be and conceivably always is so partial, fluctuating, occasional, ambiguous, vague, or otherwise indistinct or unclear as to preclude a's articulation of what is disclosed in any way that could count as evidence to him or others of what x is like in general. Moreover, my knowing that I have access to x is quite distinct from my knowing or even having good reason to believe that one interpretation of x is preferable to another. I may in reading a murder mystery have access to all the information I need in order to name the murderer, yet not be able to shape this information in such a way as to make the identification obvious. To these problems and others we shall return in a moment.

First, however, we need to get a bit clearer about the sense of the cartographically technical term 'evidence'. Let me introduce it as follows. Evidence is a polyadic relation of the general form: e is evidence to someone a for some thesis p. This relation applies to something x disclosed in the life of a, the articulation of which may serve as a ground for a's holding p. More precisely: necessarily, e is evidence to a for p if and only if

(i) a has access to something x
(ii) x is in some respect articulable by a as e
(iii) e has the status of being a reasonable ground for a's holding p.

This use of 'evidence' is introduced so as to apply to all theses indiscriminately, but it has relevant application in our discussion to theses regarding the nature of reality, whether they be those of a pretheoretical or theoretical sort. The ontologist may, for example, have evidence for his conclusions regarding survey as well as theory, given, of course, that conclusions at the level of survey are at all legitimate within the ontological enterprise. An investigation guided by the question "What is reality?" provides evidence only insofar as the investigator has access to something the articulation of which can serve as a good reason for his holding the view that reality is such and so. It is, I suppose, logically possible that an *x* to which the investigator has access is not itself reality or a part of it, so that its providing evidence of reality would be in some important sense only circumstantial. It is also logically possible that, though the *x* be reality or a part of it, the access to it and hence the evidence for a view of *x* provided by it are indirect. These are different cases and worth keeping distinct. Obviously, the logical possibility remains that both access and the evidence it provides are direct. We cannot avoid interest in each of these possibilities, even though how they might be illustrated may remain enigmatic. This much might be said, however. If someone *a* has access to reality and reports upon what is disclosed directly or indirectly to him through that access, then *b*, who does not enjoy that access, may, other conditions perhaps being fulfilled, take his own access to *a*'s report as providing evidence to him, *b*, for a certain view of reality. Such evidence would be circumstantial for that view. Thus, what serves as evidence for one investigator does not necessarily serve as evidence to another, though its report might.

This allows us to emphasize the point that evidence counts as such only relative to a certain person. This relativity rests upon the condition that evidence is a reasonable ground or good reason, not for the truth of *p*, but for someone's holding *p*. Reasons why something is true and reasons why someone ought to hold something to be true are different sorts of reasons. It should also be made clear that this condition on evidence does not presuppose that someone actually holds *p* to be true. I may have evidence for *p* but in fact hold a contrary view *q*; I hold the view I do in spite of the evidence.

The epistemic question of the conditions on my knowing or justifiably believing *p* on the basis of evidence must attend to the issues, not only of whether I do believe *p* and whether I do indeed have evidence for that belief, but whether I know or believe that I have this evidence and, further, know or believe that it is evidence for my holding *p*. Clearly, I may "have" evidence for holding *p*, whether I in fact believe *p* or not, without knowing or believing that I do. Such epistemic issues are important, but I shall tiptoe around them, for I shall phrase my question in terms of whether I can have evidence for a view of reality, rather than in terms of whether I can know or be justified in believing that my holding of such a view is justified.

It should also be obvious from what has been said that *a*'s "having" evidence for holding *p* does not presuppose *a*'s actual articulation of it. In a "strong" sense of 'evidence' we might want to say that *x* must not only be articulable by *a* as *e*, but in fact articulated by *a*; only thus, we might say, does one "fully" have it. But I wish to use the term 'evidence' in such a way that both "articulated evidence" and "unarticulated evidence" can be had by a. This is a terminological decision which will cause no harm so long as we respect it.

But now the point must be emphasized that a's having access to something x does not of itself provide a with evidence about x. If the disclosure of x is such as to preclude either any articulation of it by a or an articulation which is such as to provide reasonable grounds for a's holding p, then it fails to provide evidence for p. Here the elements of (a) the articulability of x by a, (b) the status of being a reasonable ground, and (c) the status of the thesis which one may hold on such grounds needs further discussion.

To begin with (c), what might serve as evidence for one sort of thesis may not serve for another. Consider two sorts of thesis, a pretheoretic thesis having to do with the general traits of reality as surveyed logically prior to the construction of a theory and a theoretic thesis which, also having to do with reality, may be included within a theory or system which has been constructed. The example, it can be seen, has to do with different investigative levels at which theses may be considered. It may well be that the sort of articulation of some aspect or part of x which could serve as evidence for theses at the investigatively lower level is different from the sort which could serve at the higher. This is, as we have had occasion to see in our discussion of the ontological enterprise, exactly the case. The manner of articulation must be fitted to the needs of the manner of thesis. In particular, the move from survey to theory must, if it is to provide evidence for theory, assume that what is gleaned from survey can be formulated both without reference to theory and yet in such a way as to illustrate the categories and principles of theory.

Consider, for example, Berkeley's view that things of everyday perception which are vulgarly called material objects are to be theoretically understood as collections of ideas. We ought, he thinks, to "think" in the properly theoretical fashion about such matters, but it will not harm us to "speak" in the vulgar. Now, it is not the case that for Berkeley everyday perception distorts or falsifies reality; it does provide us with access to reality. But it is Berkeley's view, as I understand it, that the articulation in the vulgar of what is disclosed does not of itself provide a reasonable ground for the proper theoretic understanding of it. That sort of articulation of reality is not fitted to serve as evidence for the proper sort of theory of it. It is not that that sort of articulation is incorrect or even misleading, for, given the appropriate rules of explanation, it is quite acceptable; it is, rather, that it is, of itself, unavailable as evidence for theory, whether of the limited categoreal scheme or the larger ontological system itself. This may serve as an illustration of how one sort of articulation at a lower level may be seen by one philosopher to be opaque to the needs of a higher level. We may, of course, still ask a question of Berke-ley, namely, whether there is any sort of pretheoretic articulation of everyday perception which can serve as evidence for his own theory. Frankly, I do not think that he is able to come up with anything. It seems to me that it is only on a certain theoretically directed reinterpretation of everyday perception, i.e., by the application of a strong filter, that he is able to frame such evidence. But this is to beg the issue or rather to load the dice. He has to emasculate appearing of its disclosive dimension from the beginning, to reduce it, that is, to the datal and the significative.

Here we move to a consideration of (b) "reasonable grounds." They are—and therefore evidence is—of two sorts. First, there may be grounds for holding that a certain thesis has wide interpretive range, i.e., is broadly adequate and explanatory. In the case of ontology, evidence of this sort would be logically posterior to the provision of a theory, though inde-pendent of theory in its articulation. For the sake of brevity, we may refer to this sort of evidence as that of adequation. One's access to reality would have to provide an indefinite range of disclosures which, nontheo-retically articulated, serve as a good reason for inclining him towards holding that the theory was adequate. Note that such evidence is evi-dence of adequacy only if it is provided by access, i.e., disclosure of things as they really are. And in order to establish such, to "know" that adequacy is being legitimately tested, one must be able to establish that disclosure is a genuine case of access on grounds independent of theory.

The second sort of reasonable ground and hence of evidence is that of the provision of a structure which can serve the A-condition of preroga-tive fit, as well as a cue for the construction of a theory. Again, such a ground rests upon access; it enters into the ontological enterprise at a level logically prior to and independent of theory construction. One must, that is, have grounds for thinking that a certain articulation or range of articulations of a part of reality to which one has pretheoretic access provides a structure to which the structure of the categoreal scheme must directly (i.e., without application of rules of interpretation) conform to some extent. I shall discuss more carefully the use of such terms as 'fit' and 'favored for fit' in the next section. The important point at this juncture is that such an articulation of structure must be such as to be *available* for theoretic fit. And again, the availability is relative to the sort of thesis or theory in question.

We are now in a position to understand (a), the condition of articula-bility. The point is simple. That which is disclosed in access can be evi-dential only if it can be propositionally characterized in such a manner that the characterization is supportive, to some degree and in some man-ner, of some thesis which the investigator might entertain. A characterization counts as articulation only so long as it has this supportive force. Thus, in regard to evidence for (or against) any theory regarding reality, the constraints upon articulation may be spelled out as follows. The characterization of that aspect of reality which is disclosed must be both (1) neutral to the application of theoretical notions in general, whether of one theory or any of its possible rivals, and (2) available for the purposes of supporting (or counting against) some ontological theory or other in some manner and to some degree. Condition (1) has been sufficiently discussed. It is (2) which needs a closer look.

The manners of support are, as we have seen, two, i.e., an articulation may support an ontological theory in the role of either adequation or fit. It is the latter of these upon which we have come to focus our interest. Articulated evidence which serves to provide for prerogative fit or to cue us into the construction of an ontological theory must, then, consist of a characterization of accessively disclosed reality which is available for fit. Specifically, it must provide a characterization of the *structure* of that which is disclosed to which the structure of a categoreal scheme *can* be fitted. Precisely what is involved in regard to the fitting of the latter to the former is a topic of the next two sections. For the present I want merely to make some observations regarding characterizability in general.

Characterization for the purpose of theoretic availability cannot be such as to do violence to that which is characterized. It cannot be imposed on a recalcitrant material and it cannot be so selective or abstractive in regard to the overall shape of that material as to misrepresent what appears as it appears. Should the material be amorphous or fuzzy or should it be constitutively ambiguous, the characterization must itself report those features. This is not to say, of course, that the characterization must itself be vague or ambiguous, but rather that what is vague or ambiguous must be reported as such. The characterization, for example, that x is ambiguous between m and n is itself ambiguous only if the terms 'm' and 'n' are ambiguous. One can conceivably be clear about the nebulous, the vague, the faint, the ephemeral. The point that needs to be made, then, is that the adoption in theory of a category or principle of specified alternativeness or vagueness could be evidentially supported only by a clear characterization. In a nutshell, an inability to clearly characterize a disclosure is in fact an inability to characterize in an available manner. The mystic who finds his encounter with "God" to be ineffable gives us nothing of any theoretic significance about "God," whether the ineffability be due to his own or an avowed generically human deficiency or to the contrariness of the appearing itself. Indeed, any encounter or disclosure to which one responds by saying that nothing clear can be said about it or that "one must experience" it in order to catch on to what one does say about it is unavailable for the theoretic by default. Access to reality is of no ontological interest whatsoever unless it can be articulated.

Clarity of characterization is always necessary for evidential support; the clarity of what is characterized sometimes is. There is a limit to the theoretical usefulness of clear characterizations of the unclear. In particular, a structure of the disclosed may be made available for fit only if it is sufficiently determinate of itself to count as a genuine structure. Fit, then, requires not only clarity of characterization, but significant clarity in the characterized. We may now attempt to be more precise about this.

6. To acknowledge a *fit* between sets of material x and y is to acknowledge that both x and y exhibit an identical structure among their elements. A fit between x (e.g., a categoreal scheme) and y (e.g., a set of disclosures), then, presupposes that (i) there is an articulable structure s of x and an articulable structure s' of y, such that (ii) s is identical to s'.

It follows on these conditions that the relation of fit is symmetrical and reflexive, but it does not follow that it is transitive. This brings out the important fact that fit is relative to a specifiable structure. Of course, a relation of "perfect fit" would be transitive if we mean by it that x fits y in virtue of their "proper and complete" structures, whatever that could be. I have problems about the notion of the proper and complete structure of something. Not only might we distinguish levels of structure, from first-level through an indefinite hierarchy of metastructures, but we may also distinguish alternative articulations of structure, rival readings so to speak. Moreover, the possibility must be allowed that at least some subject-matters are inexhaustible in their discoverable characteristics and that, therefore, the full articulation of their structures is incorrigibly incomplete.

Given the fact that any subject-matter x may be more or less generally characterized, the articulated structure of x by virtue of which it may be fitted to y may be so extremely general as to serve to fit x to a wide range of alternatives to y. Consider two contrary categoreal schemes a and b. It is possible that, whereas a certain structure s of a set of disclosures x is shared only by a, a certain more general structure s' of x which is exemplified by s is shared by b as well. It follows that both a and b fit x, though we would want to say that they do so unevenly.

Similarly, on the same sense of 'fits', each of rival categoreal schemes a and b may fit the same disclosure x relative to different structures of x which, whether at the same level of generality or not, are selected from different aspects or regions of x. Consider, for example, a structure s of x which contains substructures s_1 and s_2. It is entirely possible that a fits x only in respect to s_1, whereas b fits x only in respect to s_2.

These tendencies towards promiscuity in the application of the notion of fit derive from the inherent relativity of the notion to the specification of the relevant structure. We might attempt to bring this fact to greater clarity by construing fit as a three-term relation. We might say that a claim of the form 'x fits y' is systematically indeterminate as it stands, and can be made determinate only by substitution of a claim of the form 'x fits y in respect to s'. We thereby gain transitivity.

So much for the notion of fit. But now we need to take account of the possibility that, though x does not fit y in respect to s, it comes close to doing so. Identity of structure is thus denied in favor of similarity. This is important because, insofar as we are concerned with evidential force, we may, all things being equal, take closeness of similarity of structure as evidence for deciding between rival theories. Rival categoreal schemes a and b may each fit a certain structure s' of x, yet a may come closer than b to fitting a structure s of x of which s' is only a part, aspect, or generalization. In general, given a revealed structure s which is taken to be evidentially significant, it may be that rival categoreal schemes come more or less close to fitting it. Perhaps we ought to introduce the notion of "better fits in respect to s" to mark this recognition of being closer to being identical in structure. But this latter is, theoretically speaking, an unwieldy notion. Degrees of similarity, once recognized, can be theoretically honored, but it is not at all clear how they can be theoretically explained except by some device of enumerating identities. Being "close to identical" might then cash out as being identical in many respects. Unfortunately, this approach has a limit to its applicability which is quite devastating in regard to evidential force. For to "cash out" a judgment that x better fits y than does z in respect to s in terms of x's sharing more identities of structure with y than does z in respect to s is to assume that s is unequivocally articulable in terms of a certain set of determinate substructures, each of which has equal value for the purposes of counting. Further, if one assumes that this additive process provides a means of determining the level of evidential force, then the value accorded each substructure for the purpose of counting must correspond to an increment of evidential force. But there seems to be no respectable way of supporting such a correspondence except by appeal to the principles of a certain theory. This is clearly question-begging, for it involves a manner of articulation of that which is disclosed which is not itself theoretically neutral. The upshot is that the notion of "better fits in respect to s" cannot, if it is to do evidential work, be interpreted in terms of identities. It has to be a notion of cartographical import, one which has legitimacy by answering to a recognition of similarity at the pretheoretic level.

The problem is not insurmountable. It involves the specification of a variation upon "fitting" which is not relative to a specified structure and which takes account of the pretheoretically recognized axes of comparison of width, specificity, and similarity. It comes to this. Letting x stand for a set of disclosures of reality and a and b for rival categoreal schemes, then

> a better fits x than does b if and only if the widest and most specific articulable structure of a is more similar to the widest and most specific articulable structure of x than is the widest and most specific articulable structure of b.

This formulation allows the introduction of degrees of fittingness by means of a series of comparisons in regard to greater or lesser similarity. It also allows of refinements in regard to the variation of conditions along one or the other axes of width and specificity. Thus, one might find one categoreal scheme to be better fitting than another along the axis of width but not that of specificity. Which is to say that, of two schemes, one may have a greater claim to width while the other has greater claim to depth.

We can now introduce the important notion of *being favored for fit*. Here we must recall three things. First, there may be diverse avenues of access by means of which reality is disclosed in different domains or in different aspects. Second, for the purposes of evidence, what is disclosed must be articulable in a manner which makes what is articulated available in some evidential role. Third, for the purposes of evidence in the role of fit, what is disclosed must be an articulable structure. Evidence that is favored for fit, then, must be an articulation of structure which derives from an avenue of access which is itself favored, i.e., an avenue for the accessive priority of which persuasive reasons can be given.

It is not necessarily decisive in the adjudication between rival categoreal schemes a and b that a better fits a certain region of reality x, as disclosed by an avenue of access m, than b, for there may be another avenue of access n which is favored over m and which discloses a region of reality y which b better fits than a. It is the theme of this work that there is a favored avenue of access—and a highly favored one—which discloses a structure of things. This order, then, is, if sufficiently articulable for evidential purposes, favored for fit and, all other things being equal, that categoreal scheme which is so constructed as to better fit it than another is to be considered as better supported and, hence, more likely to be true of reality.

Thus far, we have discussed "better fitting" and "being favored for fit" on the model of adjudicating between two rival categoreal schemes which have already been formulated. We have, that is, been discussing matters as though we were comparing rival schemes by reference to the A-condition of prerogative fit. But our interest lies less with this sort of situation than with that of contriving a categoreal scheme in the first place. The evidence we are concerned with is that of providing a cue for construction, and therefore our interest falls upon *a process of fitting* a scheme under construction *to* a certain set of disclosures. More specifically, given a structure which is favored for fit, the task of interest is that of guiding our speculative imagination, prompting and checking it at every phase of construction, by the device of choosing, among all the alternatives with which our imagination may supply us, those which, in regard to each specified constructive issue, better fits that structure. There are other tests of constructive success, of course, which also have to be considered, among them being that of adequacy to a wider range of evidence than that supplied by favored access alone. And this means that the process of "fitting to" may not be decisive in regard to our choices. But the function of a cue is not to be decisive in any case, but rather intuitive. A cue is a lure, an aid, a guide.

We may now attempt to shed some light on the nature of a structure in general and the nature of an ontologically available structure in particular.

7. The technical term 'structure' is introduced here at the cartographical level, for it must apply, not only to theories, but to pretheoretic orderings. If a system at the theoretic level of investigation is to be fitted, by virtue of its structure, to a certain range of disclosures at the pretheoretic level, by virtue of its structure, then we must allow that, in spite of the differences at those different levels in their origination, their investigative roles, their manners of applicability, and their conditions of acceptability, they nonetheless must be characterizable as *structural* in exactly the same sense. This point might be put like this. The structure of a subject-matter, whether that subject-matter be a system or a range of presystemic disclosures, is exhibited only by abstracting from its investigative context. It may be useful, then, to get at what is involved in a structure as such by comparing pretheoretic and theoretic candidates for exhibiting a structure and bracketing out the contextual differences involved. For this we may concentrate on the four contextual considerations of origin, role, application, and acceptability.

To begin with origin, it is enough to observe that the one sort of structure is elicited from the disclosures of a purported avenue of access, a stance, at the pretheoretic level of their appearing, whereas the other sort is posited as a product of speculative proposal. The pretheoretic structure is "lifted out" from a given embodiment of it, whereas the theo-

retic structure is "introduced" for application to an independently specified material. The difference between the two processes is striking and
important, but the point to be made here is that neither process is to be
considered as an element in the structure which is processed. In fact,
nothing rules out the possibility that the same structure may be involved
in both processes.

The roles to be played in the investigation by these two structures are,
as I have already discussed at length in chapter 2, very different indeed. A
presystemic structure may, given that it derives from a favored access to
reality, serve two possible roles, namely, that of providing a test of prerogative fit for eventual adjudication between rival systems and that of
providing a cue for system construction. A theoretic structure may be
said to serve two sorts of roles, namely, the systemic role of providing an
intelligible order within the system as a whole (as, for example, by exhibiting the conformity of the system to the BOP) and the various metasystemic roles which are carried forward in the diverse metasystemic
claims regarding the system (as, for example, in the R-claim: if a system is
claimed to be true of R, then it is claimed to be true in all of its parts or
dimensions, including its structure). The fact remains that each of these
diverse roles in the investigation is a role of something, viz., a structure,
which is identifiable apart from that or any other role it may be expected
to play. And nothing rules out the possibility that the same structure may
play diverse roles in the same investigation.

Both a pretheoretic and a theoretic structure can be said to have an
"application" to a subject-matter. But the manners of application involved
are very different. The pretheoretic structure "applies" to the subject-
matter from which it is elicited and in which it is embodied; it comes
with its application already in place. The structure does not stand in need
of an interpretation in terms of concrete appearances. Of course, once a
structure has been elicited from a certain range of disclosures it may
then be considered apart from that range and perhaps subsequently provided with an interpretation in terms of another range. This serves to un-
derline the fact that the manner of the original application of any structure, however arrived at, is irrelevant to its being the structure it is, even
though it deserves to be called a structure only if it can be said to be a
structure which is applicable to some subject-matter. Now, a theoretic
structure does stand in need of interpretation, for it does not come with
an application ready-made. Since, however, the actual interpretation
which might be given it is not to be taken as part of it, the theoretic structure can only be understood as something about which some manner of
interpretation or other can be given. This claim of interpretability, just as
the claim of applicability in regard to pretheoretic structures, is an inte-

gral part of the structure itself. This point is made clearer perhaps by re-calling what was said about systems in section 2 of chapter 2. It was pro-posed there that a system is to be understood as an interpreted schema. If, then, we delete the actual interpretation, we are left with a schema (an ordering of terms for entities) and the bare claim that that schema can be given an interpretation. The assumption is that, though what is to count as a structure is not to be determined relative to some specific subject-matter, every structure must be, after all, a proposed structure of some-thing or other. If a formal scheme of terms and relations is not proposed as being a structure of anything, then it is not properly to be called a structure; it is just an abstract pattern or scheme. (This is not, of course, intended to denigrate the importance of abstract schemes, for they may be employed in any number of useful ways. For example, such normative schemes as those involved in decision procedures, programs, devices of calculation, and reasoning are not easily understood as structures of any-thing, except perhaps an ideal process or state of affairs which can be identified only by their means.) We may consider the structure of an *on-tological* system, then, to be identical to the categoreal scheme and the claim that rules of explanation for it are formulable (together with, if it is relevant, the bare statement that one or more integrity provisions are in-cluded in the system). This suggests a minimal characterization for any structure as consisting of just this: a specification of order among entities as being of certain sorts, i.e., considered in general or as cases, together with a claim that this ordering of entities is applicable in some determi-nate but unspecified way to some (unspecified) subject-matter.

That the conditions on the acceptability of a structure are not to be taken as parts of the structure considered seems obvious. Thus the A-conditions discussed in chapter 2 need not be discussed here in regard to their relevance, if any, to pretheoretic structures. But two of them, namely, consistency and coherence, may seem to suggest conditions on something's being a structure at all. I do not think a case can be made for coherence, however. Certainly a pretheoretic structure need not be co-herent in order to be a structure, for we do not demand coherence in the limited but only in the comprehensive view of things. Moreover, it seems overly protective of ontology to demand that any structure which is proposed as ontological must be coherent in order merely to be con-sidered as an ontological proposal; we just want to say that it is perhaps not the best ontological proposal if it lacks coherence. Consistency poses a tougher issue. It does seem that we expect from the beginning that any-thing proposed as a structure is itself consistent in some important sense of that term. Perhaps the point is that, apart from consistency among its elements, we can't tell what we have. And it seems obvious that an ontological system which either fits or is adequate to an inconsistent structure must itself be inconsistent and thus entirely unacceptable.

I will take this unexplicated and perhaps ultimately intuitively understood condition of consistency to be built into the notion of "order." With this in mind we may continue to specify a structure as (a) a specification of an order among (b) a specification of sorts of entities about which (c) applicability to some determinate subject-matter may be claimed. To this we may now add that (d) the terms and ordering devices of the structure must be sufficiently unambiguous and intuitively clear to allow application. The point of this addition is obvious.

This general characterization of a structure is about as far as we should go with it, for any more specific characterization of what are to count as terms and ordering devices would only serve to indicate a certain type of structure or level of its complexity. It is, for example, possible to distinguish *functional* and *nonfunctional* types of structure. The hallmark of the former is the purely functional standing of its terms and the consequent primitiveness of ordering devices, typically relations. It has sometimes been said that the thrust of the development of theoretical enterprises throughout their history, whether in philosophy, science, or whatever, has been to realize the purity of explanation by means of functional system, an ideal which provides for individuality only as a function of order. I am not at all convinced that this is a correct reading of history, though I suspect that it is quite appropriate to the development of some theoretical pursuits during the modern period, those of contemporary physics in particular. In any event, it is certainly not the case that every articulated structure is functional. Any ordered arrangement of elements of a putative subject-matter which, considered by itself, assumes the primacy of individuals or kinds within the subject-matter must be, if at all applicable to those aspects of the subject-matter, nonfunctional in essence. Thus, a classificatory order need not involve the application of a functional structure. Given dogs and men, one may order them under the kind animals without assuming, for example, that a man is to be understood merely as an animal which is not a dog. Clearly, most of our day-to-day orderings are nonfunctional in this technical sense.

In addition, structures may differ in *complexity*. At the simplest and most abstract level, a structure may be said to consist of two sorts of entities about which nothing more is said than that they stand in a certain unspecified but nonsymmetrical relation to each other. To specify anything further about this relation but not about its terms would be to propose a simple functional structure. As the number of terms and relations are increased, the structure may be said to become "wider;" as the terms or relations are more specifically characterized, the structure may be said to become "thicker."

The *scope* of a structure is not intrinsic to it; rather, it is limited by the subject-matter to which it is claimed to be applicable. Such claims can, of course, be enlarged or diminished, and such is often the fate of a structure after its initial proposal. It is seen to be more broadly or more narrowly applicable than originally thought. Strictly speaking, only ontological systems are proposed as comprehensive of quite everything, though systems of universal science may be proposed as comprehensive of life. However, it should be remembered that each are proposed only at a certain high level of generality and without applicability to unspecified differences of detail within the subject-matter. In any event, it is useful to emphasize the logical independence of the claimed scope and the functional or nonfunctional nature of a structure. This is important for our project, for an ontological system, which is such as to claim comprehensiveness both in regard to its coincidence with a designated subject-matter which is itself taken to be comprehensive and its adequacy to life in its totality (i.e., is such as to claim to cover "everything," in both the ontological and the more broadly referential sense of 'everything'), need not be taken to be functional in nature. I can see no good reason for assuming that functionality is to be included among either the S-conditions or the O-conditions. Moreover, it hardly seems reasonable to presume that functionality is a condition on the success or acceptability of an ontological system. The only reason I can imagine why anyone would think so is that it is assumed that modern physical science (on a certain functionalistic undertanding of it of course) provides the model for ontological inquiry. But this assumption represents, it seems, either a presystemic assumption of the identification of proper ontology and modern science or an engrained pretheoretic presumption of the favor to be accorded to a theoretical and, more specifically, scientific access to reality. I have trouble seeing how even a respectable case could be made for either of these views. On the other hand, the mere fact of the logical independence of a claim of comprehension and the functional nature of a system does not rule out the possibility that the best ontological system will turn out to be a functional one. But, of course, neither does it preclude the possibility that it will turn out to be nonfunctional.

I must admit that I have a special reason for thinking that an acceptable ontological system will not be functional. My reason is this. I wish to propose the practical stance as the favored access to reality and the structure of the practical arena as providing a cue to ontological construction. But it seems to me that the structure which can be elicited from the practical arena is not and cannot be construed as functional in nature. Why I believe these things will emerge in the next two chapters. But the point to be made here is that a closeness or significant similarity between non-functional and functional structures seems out of the question.

8. Ideally, a structure which is ontologically favored for fit would conform to the following conditions. (1) It would be a structure which is disclosed through a favored access to reality. (2) It would be so articulable at the pretheoretic level as to be available for comparison with categoreal schemes in regard to greater or lesser fit. (3) A claim to comprehensive scope can be made in its behalf without doing violence to its nature, i.e., it is expandable in such a way as to comprehend a world.

I have said enough about the justifications for conditions (1) and (2). Condition (3) derives from the fact that a structure which is accepted as limited in scope from the beginning, as unexpandable beyond the borders of its specific subject-matter, cannot be assumed on any grounds to provide a basis for the construction of a comprehensive system. It could at best be taken as an alert and in no case other than a piece of evidence for adequation or explanation. By saying that such a structure must be expandable to comprehensiveness, I want to indicate two things: first, that it need not (and surely will not) be such as to be already fitted for that scope and, second, that consequently it must be capable of some sort of nonspoiling, integrity-preserving, but adjustive consideration and manipulation in the course of ontological inquiry. That this must be the case seems to me to be clear; how its possibility is to be understood, how it is to be illustrated, is not so clear. But the brute fact of the matter is this. The structure which may be elicited from the diclosures of one avenue of access or stance will not be in part or in whole identical to the structures disclosed from all other stances. The oppositional structures of the theoretical and the practical stances rule that out immediately. To see this, all we have to do is to remind ourselves of the differing terrains of each. The practical arena and the theoretical field are so unlike each other in terms of their occupants and the relations among them as to provide us with a very paradigm of contrast. For examples, the stancer and the "relation" of stancing must be included in one but cannot be included in the other. Thus, the attempt to stretch the structure elicited from one stance so as to cover or include those of all other stances is to attempt the impossible. Yet, the fact remains that an ontological system, including its structure, must claim and be tested by its success in a comprehensive applicability to all of life, including all of its disclosures and their structures. It seems clear, then, that the claim to the comprehensive applicability of an acceptable ontological system cannot be satisfied if the structure of that system is exactly the same as that of any stance-relative range of disclosures. And it follows, it would seem, that a pretheoretic structure which is to be taken as a cue must be such that it is patient of being considered under alterations which both derive from the concern for comprehension and yet allow for the preservation of that integrity of the original structure which its employment as a cue, as a product of favored access, presupposes.

So much may be said at this juncture about these conditions of favored derivation, availability, and comprehensive expandability. I will have a bit more to say about them and their application to the structure of the practical arena in the last chapter.

9. I would like in closing to emphasize the limited role of favored access in ontological investigation.

An access to reality in our lives is favored over another only if its disclosure of reality is in some respect more likely to be true of the way things really are than the other. I take this to be the case for the practical stance. I want to say that what is disclosed from the practical stance is *in a certain respect* to be ontologically favored. I do not want to say that every appearance disclosed by the practical stance has a claim to be taken more seriously in every respect than any appearance disclosed through any other stance or manner of appearing. To be still more specific, I do not want to maintain that the disclosures of the practical stance could ever be justifiably taken as having greater evidential force in the role of adequation. And this is because, whether one takes the practical stance as favored or not, favored access cannot by the nature of the case have anything to do with adequation.

Consider. On the one hand, it is the aim of an ontological system to apply to, cover, be adequate to everything in life. On the other hand, no ontological system need apply to the disclosures of avenues of access which are ontologically barren, i.e., to disclosures of a subject-matter which does not fall within the domain of reality. Assuming both of these hands, we are thus led to the conclusion that there are no ontologically barren disclosures, which is to say that all roads lead to reality. This conclusion sits comfortably with an assumption which we have made, namely, that, since all appearing is necessarily part of life and since life is itself thoroughly real, each and every aspect or dimension of appearing *per se* is a part of reality. This assumption may be denied. And the assumptions upon which it rests, somewhat loosely to be sure, may also be denied. But unless it is assumed, the condition on a system of adequacy to every item of life would seem to me to be without persuasiveness.

The point of the condition of adequacy is that every item of life, insofar as it is articulable, has equal evidential weight in confirming or disconfirming the covering role of the system. It makes no difference at all whether one holds the strange view that the items of life have different degrees of reality. Suppose I were to say (though I cannot imagine what I would mean by saying it) that the disclosures of the practical stance have a "greater degree of reality" than those of the theoretical stance. This cannot be taken as indicating that an ontological system should favor those disclosures over others. The point of an ontological system is not to honor the best of reality, but to grasp it all, to cover even the least. A system which distinguished between higher and lower degrees of reality would still have to be adequate to everything, both the higher-degree stuff and the lower-degree stuff. An ontologist must be completely democratic when he sets outs to test for adequacy.

The notion of favored access is of no earthly use in regard to the determination of the adequacy of an ontological theory. In regard to cuing and prerogative fit, however, things are of quite another stripe. Here the notion of favored access is of essential significance, not with respect to any favor to be granted the appearances *per se,* but with respect to the favor to be granted the structure disclosed in the appearances. It is the structure disclosed which has favor, not the appearance *per se* of that structure, for any structure *qua* appearance, whatever the avenue of access and however much it may claim or have claimed for its comprehensiveness, is just another item over which a system is to stretch its blanket. All of this should be old hat by now. But the upshot is that favored access can only be to some domain of reality disclosive of a structure to which the structure of the system may be fitted. It has to do with structure conforming to structure, not item covering item.

Part 2

The Practical Arena

♦♦♦

5

The Primacy of the Practical

♦♦♦ 1. I will now argue for the thesis that practical stancing is to be favored for ontological purposes over any other manner of access to reality in our lives. The first part of my argument will have the following simple structure:

(1) Practical stancing has primacy in our lives.
(2) Practical stancing provides access to reality.
(3) If any manner of access to reality has primacy in our lives, it provides the only favored access to reality in our lives.
Therefore,
(4) Practical stancing provides the only favored access to reality in our lives.

Let me call this the *basic argument*. Subsidiary arguments in support of each premise will comprise the substance of this chapter.

This is, as I say, only a part of the argument, for the favor concluded is not yet shown to be a favor which is available for ontological purposes. As indicated in the last two sections of the previous chapter, an appeal to favored access can play a significant role in ontology only by virtue of its disclosure of a structure which is favored for fit and therefore available for the theoretic applications involved in both the A-condition of prerogative fit and a cue for the constructing of a system. In addition to the conclusion above, then, it must be shown both (i) that there is a structure of the practical arena which can be elicited from the disclosures of practical stancing and (ii) that that structure is so articulable as to be available and appropriately expandable for theoretic purposes. I will address these two further conditions in turn in the next two chapters.

2. Premise (1) in the basic argument abbreviates the claim that, of all manners of stancing or being oriented to things, only the general manner of practical stancing enjoys a certain priority in our day-by-day living. The sort of priority involved is one which is exhibited in reflection upon the course of our lives and without bias towards any specialized form of ordering which may be derived from some specific manner of stancing. Obviously, no sort of priority which is distinctively practical, theoretical, aesthetic, or otherwise stance-bound can be at issue. For example, that practical stancing may enjoy some sort of "practical priority" over theoretical stancing and may fail to enjoy some sort of "theoretical priority" over theoretical stancing is hardly of interest to us here. What is at issue is something broader, applicable across different stances, and of *vital* significance.

Let me illustrate what I have in mind. It is already apparent from previous discussions that the practical stance enjoys priority over the theoretical in at least three ways. It is pretheoretical in origin, its presence is a necessary condition for the initiation of the theoretical stance, and its sovereignty is apparent throughout the sustaining of the theoretical stance. From the first of these priorities, it would seem to follow that practical stancing is, in its very nature, independent of anything theoretical. From the second and third we can conclude that the opposite is not true; the very possibility of the theoretical rests upon the power of the practical, both as regards initiating agency and sustaining tolerance. The third priority, which is most important for us here, allows us to see the relationship between the two as one of dominance; the practical stance is the finally compelling one. No matter how absorbing the theoretical, if, for example, it becomes painful for one to sit any longer in a certain way or if it becomes very desirable to urinate, then the practical situation and our awareness of it comes to the fore, at first distracting from and perhaps distorting of the course of theoretical attention and finally, perhaps, disallowing it altogether. Plato understood this well and wished it were otherwise. But in our lives as we live them—or in any life insofar as I can make sense out of what living can come to—it is not otherwise. The looming insistency of the practical is, to put it bluntly, simply a fact of life.

But now it can be seen that this last manner of the priority of practical stancing, its sovereignty, applies not only to the theoretical, but universally. The practical stance is, whatever else, common coin among all men, not as something we merely lapse into from time to time, but as something which is irremediable, autocratic in its insistency, insidiously presumptive. This fact of the tenacious and brooding sovereignty of the practical stance throughout one's life is what I wish to indicate by the phrase "the primacy of the practical."

It is important to keep in mind what is at issue in this conclusion. We are concerned about the relative place of the diverse manners of stancing in our lives, not the relative influence in our lives of the diverse products and ingredients of those manners. One can make the case (though I cannot imagine how one can do so persuasively) that in our lives today, even in our ordinary practical affairs, the products of theoretical concern—and perhaps of science in particular—have achieved a dominating role. A similar and perhaps even stronger case can be made for the influence upon the course of our practical deliberations and decisions of such other cultural factors as religion, historical lore, and socio-political custom. But such considerations are quite beside the point of the relative dominance in our lives of the manners of stancing themselves. For, if I am right, it is because of the primacy of the practical that such beliefs, theories, customs, "truths," and so on as may be derived from these other areas have the importance they do in our lives.

I do not think that further argument in support of the primacy claim is needed. The fact is stark. An attempt to understand why it is a fact is a further issue, of course, and one which need not concern us at this level. Nonetheless, it seems to me that we are justified in expanding upon the sovereignty of practical stancing in such a way as to aid such understanding. So long as we recognize that the acceptance of this more expansive picture is not needed to ensure the fact of primacy, we will, I think, find it illuminating to consider it.

The expansion is this. Throughout our lives, at least insofar as we can be said to achieve and preserve some orientation from day to day and situation to situation, practical stancing is not merely sovereign in an ever-present potentiality, so to speak, but is actually present in a background and controlling manner.

This picture presupposes that view of appearing, indicated in chapter 4, according to which a focal and selective awareness is present within a broader and nonfocal awareness of the sort which Ortega y Gasset has called *contar con,* counting on (*SLM* 48–49). Thus, as I write, my attention is focused upon the marks on a page and on what I am to put down on that page, but I am equally aware, though nonfocally, of the pen in my hand, the chair upon which I sit, the room in which I work. These things are there for me; their presence is something I orient myself in terms of, rely on, take myself to be together with. There is, I should make clear, no notion of an "unconscious," "subconscious," or "preconscious" here, either in some substantive or merely functional sense. (I have always, I must confess, had trouble understanding what such things might come to.) If consciousness is taken to be coextensive with awareness, then we are as conscious of such "counted on" things as we are of those which we selectively attend to. Indeed, it would appear that selective focus or emphasis could only take place within a terrain which is present to one in its own distinctively "backgrounding" fashion.

The basic claim, then, is that practical stancing, which in its full-bodied presence involves a focal awareness, is always present in our lives in at least the diminished manner of involving that awareness which provides a background and that, therefore, whenever a manner of focusing which is apractical in character is present, that diminished manner of practical stancing is present as well. The secondary claim is that the background provided by practical stancing, whether that stancing is full-bodied or diminished, is the bedrock background of things upon which we count, depend, and provides thereby the range of tolerance within which the focal awareness, whether practical or apractical, is allowed its initiation, continuation, and manner of development. This provides a basis for better understanding the fact of sovereignty, the fact that one's continuing engagement upon theoretical or aesthetic stancing, say, is sometimes allowed and sometimes deflected, distorted, or even disrupted. The picture is one of symbiosis; the practical stance is the host within which the other stances are allowed their play. This must not be confused with the claim—which I take to be false—that theoretical stancing always arises within practical stancing in such a way as to serve as a means to practically determined ends. In any case, if I had argued on the basis of this claim that the practical has primacy in our lives, I would be guilty of assuming the primacy of a practical sort of ordering, namely, the practical instrumentality of means-consequences, to begin with. What is involved instead is an appeal to a tolerating presence, a presence which allows, is patient of, theoretical or other stancing focus on some occasions, but which may become intolerant on others.

This view is, I think, correct. It makes sense of our intuitions that the occasions of apractical stancing are episodic in our lives, that they require the preparation of release from the more pressing practical affairs of life, that success in sustaining the theoretical, the aesthetic, the reflective, and so on involves, not only provision of practical space for doing so, but a talent, a learned skill, for pushing the practical further into the background than it seems to demand, thereby providing some space for that theoretical or other relevent background which is conducive to success.

A final remark must be made about premise (1). It is modest in two ways. First, the claim is that practical stancing has primacy in our lives, not that it must. The reason for this is simply that, though I believe that it must, I don't know how to argue for it at the pretheoretic level. To say, as I am inclined to, that, were one to achieve such a divorce from the practical as to be locked into the theoretical, that one would no longer have a life in any genuine sense at all (having come to rest in a sort of theoretical catatonia), would appear to beg the question. Second, the claim is that practical stancing has primacy in *our* lives, not that it has primacy in some other lives which are not ours. Again, it seems patent to me that it cannot be otherwise in any life of anything anywhere at any time, but I can't imagine how to show this. All I can say is that our lives are all we have to go on and they provide us with the only models for what a life can be.

3. The general assumption (2.1), that all manners of stancing must be taken as providing access to reality, has been made and supported in previous chapters. Given (2.2), that there is a manner of stancing which is distinctively practical, premise (2) of the basic argument follows immediately. Support for (2.2) comprised a good part of chapter 1 and I shall not rehearse the relevant considerations here. Support for (2.1), however, has taken a number of forms which deserve restatement in order to make it clear that the conclusion (2) is not begged by *petitio*. The following considerations and their sources in the text will, I think, suffice.

(a) Accepting (2.1) is the way of wisdom, for there are a number of manners of stancing which are in opposition in respect to their disclosures and their reality-claims in regard to them, yet none of these reality-claims could either be self-validating or validated by appeal to a superior stance or standpoint (section 10, chapter 1).

(b) Accepting (2.1) seems to be required by the A-condition on ontological systems of adequacy to life, for, whereas there is an opposition of the diverse stances in respect to the structures disclosed of their diverse terrains and therefore strict conformity (identity) of an ontological system to any one of these structures would involve some failure of conformity to another, such a failure would seem to encourage, if not guarantee, an inadequacy of the system to some items of life (sections 8–9, chapter 4).

(c) Accepting (2.1) seems to be required by the A-condition on ontological systems of adequacy to life in all of its disclosures, for each manner of stancing is disclosive, and yet it makes no sense to require that a system which purports to be true of reality as a whole cover disclosures of a manner of stancing which provides no genuine access to reality through its disclosures (section 9, chapter 4).

But none of these sets of considerations serves to establish (2.1), for it is clear that the falsity of (2.1) and of (2) as well is consistent with each of them. Each indicates at best what it is appropriate to assume upon engagement in the ontological enterprise. A skeptic would appear to be quite justified in countering that, even if we accept every manner of appearing as itself "real," still, so far as we can know, that which is disclosed within any one such manner may well be thoroughly illusory, a complete fabrication. The logical possibility must then be allowed that at least some manners of stancing are nonaccessive of reality. I think this limited conclusion is correct, though the more radical claim that it is logically possible that our entire lives are so contrived that every manner of stancing is completely nonaccessive seems to me to be unarguable and, indeed, unimaginable. In any case, I take it that the acceptance of the mere logical possibility that (2.1) is false is no good reason for concluding that it is false. The fact is that I can think of no good reason at all for taking it to be false, whereas I have given some reasons for at least assuming it to be true.

The argument is weak. Fortunately, it is not the only argument at our disposal. Upon the assumption of (1), I think a stronger argument can be given for (2) which rests, not upon (2.1), but upon the weaker claim that at least some manners of stancing provide access to reality. The argument runs as follows:

(2.3) At least some manners of stancing provide access to reality.
(2.4) If any manner of stancing provides access to reality, practical stancing does.
Therefore, (2).

I shall not attempt to assess the merits of (2.3); I shall simply accept it as compelling on its face and turn to the consideration of support for (2.4).

My reasons for accepting this thesis are as follows. If we accept the primacy of the practical in our lives, then it would seem outrageous to maintain that, whereas some other manner of stancing is revelatory of reality to some degree or in some respect, practical stancing is totally devoid of that virtue. It is outrageous because, unable as we are to avoid recourse to the practical in our lives, the assumption of the truth of its reality-claim intrudes into our lives willy-nilly, often even in the midst of apractical stancing. Moreover, if the stronger thesis is justified and practical stancing provides an ever-present background upon which every apractical manner of stancing counts or depends, then no apractical opposition to the reality-claim of practical stancing could ever be present without there also being present the underlying assumption of that reality-claim. And surely it would be absurd to attempt to deny that which we cannot avoid assuming in the attempt.

4. But even were (2) to be found acceptable, one might still object that no good reason has been given for according favor to one manner of access to reality over any other. Why not accept each such access as equally favored? Is not this in fact the way of wisdom? The answer to this should by now be clear.

We might note first a curiosity about this proposal. It makes sense only on the assumption of (2.1); on (2.3) it becomes obscure. For only if we assume that all manners of stancing are accessive can we single out manners other than that of practical stancing for equal treatment. On (2.3) alone we are provided with no identifiable manners of access, and the addition of (2.4) allows us only to identify one such manner, namely, practical stancing. Unless some independent argument is given for the specification of a manner of access which is different from practical stancing, we will be unable to treat it as "equally favored." I know of no such independent argument.

But let us assume for the sake of argument that (2.1) is true or that we are able to identify on the basis of some argument a limited range of manners of access. Then the objection would deserve an answer, at least on a certain nonmethodological understanding of it. Let me remind you of what I said in section 1: I am not concerned in this chapter with everything that is involved in the according of favor to practical stancing for the purposes of the furtherance of ontological inquiry. The conclusion which we are after in the basic argument is therefore not that the ontologist is justified in *adopting* the hypothesis that practical stancing discloses the structure of reality more faithfully than any other manner of stancing. It is, rather, the proposal of that hypothesis itself. The objection at issue, then, is relevant to our purposes only if it is understood as indicating that no good reason has been given for the truth of (4).

Still, one might attempt to bring methodological considerations back into the evaluation of even this thesis. One might argue that the only good reason for ever adopting a thesis like (4) is that its adoption as a hypothesis serves a significant role in the furtherance of ontological inquiry. Since (4) is, after all, an ontological claim, the assessment of its warrant—or, rather, our warrant for adopting it— could only be determined by the consequences of its adoption in certain specific ontological

investigations. I have in effect already argued against this view in chapter
3. My point was that the adoption of (4) for the specific ontological purposes of providing for prerogative fit or for a cue must have pretheoretic
warrant, for, otherwise, it could not serve in those roles of adjudication
and speculative control without being question-begging, biasing in regard to theory, arbitrarily decisive. And of course the only ontological
roles at issue here in regard to the adoption of (4) are these. It follows
that the only warrant for our adopting (4) in ontological inquiry would
be that on reflective and pretheoretic consideration of the diverse manners of stancing in our day-to-day lives we have discovered grounds for
concluding that that claim is more likely to be true than not.

But have we found such grounds after all? Surely.

For since we must be content to seek them pretheoretically, in our
lives and at the level of our living them, then the only sorts of considerations which could be relevant are exactly the ones already advanced in
support of (1) and (2). And they seem not only relevant but decisive. For
if practical stancing does provide access to reality, then, even if other
manners of stancing must be taken to do so as well, the fact of the vital
priority, the sovereignty, and (if also acceptable) the constant, inexorable,
and controlling presence of practical stancing in our lives must surely incline us to its favor. These are the only sorts of reasons which could
count in favor of one manner of stancing over another, and they all count
in favor of practical stancing. Premise (3) is merely an expression of this.

6

The Structure
of the Practical Arena

♦♦♦ 1. Practical stancing is as familiar to us as everyday life. It might seem, then, that the process of eliciting the structure of its arena would be a simple and straightforward matter, involving no more than the adoption of the stance and the focusing of attention upon what is disclosed. But things are not so innocent as that, and it would be best to begin our discussion by attempting to see why not. It is to be hoped that an awareness of the difficulties which attend the task of eliciting the structure at issue will allow us, though not altogether to overcome them, nonetheless to avoid their more disturbing and distorting consequences.

The first and perhaps most obvious complication is that of achieving sufficient purity in practical stancing itself. We may as well give up any attempt to emulate the purely practical being, for, surely, such a one is as much a fiction as the purely theoretical being. We are, as are our so-called "primitive" ancestors and contemporaries, embued with culture, with custom and tradition and habituation, and educated, whether directly or indirectly, to history, theory, science, art, philosophy, and religion. That we assume a brokenly mythic view of things may also be considered likely. Of course, one does not need to live in a purely practical way in order to enjoy, within the course of life, moments of stancing which are thoroughly practical in concern and manner. The problem is that even in such moments the accrual of culture and habit cannot but be assumed to be carried forward into the very manner in which the situation is experienced. It is not just that in each occasion of practical stancing is vested the successful results of past occasions of practical stancing, but that each such occasion is funded by, weighted with, the assumptions and predilections of a larger cultural construal of things. There is, I think, no way to avoid this accrual in our lives, nor would we desire it. It follows that, if our project was to describe this or that practical situation in detail and apart from the contributions to it of specific cultural and habitual factors, we must despair of ever accomplishing our goal. Such a project would seem, in fact, to be impossible in principle, for it does not make any sense, at least so far as I can see, to construe any situation, practical or otherwise, as admitting of detailed disclosure which is free of the influence of what is carried forward in one's life and from antecedent learning and development. But, of course, this is not our project. Our concern is to get at the general structure of the practical arena as it is disclosed on any occasion of its presence and apart from the specific construal of things in particular cases. And unless we are willing to say that people from other cultures and backgrounds than our own do not engage in practical stancing at all, we must allow that there is such a general structure which is common within such stancing. What this structure comes to may indeed be very general, very spare, but it must be, in spite of that, distinctive and, thus, capable of being contrasted with other structures which are disclosed within other stances.

The weight of cultural and habitual accrual in regard to how the practical arena is disclosed to us within practical stancing is less of a threat to our project than it might at first appear. But it is a problem, for it provides us with assumptions about how things are which, though they can only be additional to the structure of the practical as such, may be mistaken as ultimate and incorrigible. This suggests that one of the bases for differing hypotheses regarding the practical arena might well be that of diverse attachments to such additive factors. It would seem that one of the dangers that confronts us is our attempting to say too much, to be too specific, about what is involved in the practical arena. And worse, since we must begin where we are, i.e., must direct the process of eliciting a structure to those occasions of practical stancing which are found in our own specifically encultured and habituated lives, and since we may be taken to share, at least to a large extent, our cultural and habitual heritage, we may come to an easy agreement on what we mistakenly take to be the structural significance of some such additive factors. Still, such possible errors derive from and are perpetuated by a sort of innocence which, in being brought to light, may be replaced by a recognition that each and every proposal regarding the structure of the practical is just a hypothesis and, thus, something subject to healthy suspicion and critical appraisal. Knowing how we might be misled in these respects will, I think, help us to avoid being so misled, at least so badly as, in our innocence, we might have been.

The same might be said of certain other difficulties which confront our project. They are insistent, but hardly unregenerate, for each may be mitigated by recognition of and constant attention to it. I have in mind four such impediments to any straightforward "reading off" of the structure of the practical arena from a consideration of the disclosures of practical stancing. Two of these have to do with the demands of survey itself and two have to do with the level of characterization desired. I will consider them in turn.

As to the activity of survey, it can never be forgotten that, though its attention to its subject-matter is pretheoretic in nature, its manner of consideration of that subject-matter is such as to prepare material for the theoretic phase of the larger investigation. This manner of consideration is, we might say, both descriptive and reportive. Thus, first, in attending to the practical arena, the aim of survey is to "describe" something which is not immediately present to the "describing" manner of attention. To make that subject-matter present is to re-present it, to bring it back before us in memory. This dislocation of the subject-matter is, of course, fraught with the dangers of bias and alien intrusion. But, again, our very awareness of this dislocation may help to keep whatever deleterious consequences it may offer to a minimum.

In the same way we can perhaps provide reins upon a certain manner of systemic intrusion. This intrusion derives from the need to employ in our reporting of the results of survey instruments of descriptive ordering and clarification. Such instruments, linguistic and conceptual, are, ideally, theoretically and systemically neutral. But it is more than easy to slip into the habits of theoretical skill; it is seductively comfortable. The rubrics of property/substance and form/matter are more than products of theoretical explanation; they are tools of clarification and description. They serve to prepare material for explanatory consideration. And clearly the provision of a characterization of the practical arena which is theoretically opaque or unusable is investigatively gratuitous. Thus, the means by which we report our findings of survey must not only be unspoiling to the subject-matter of survey at its own level, but preparatory to theoretic handling. We seem to want something impossible, an unspoiling regimentation. Again, our attention to this difficulty is our best weapon for dealing with it. And in consequence, the proper manner of reporting the structures of the practical arena is to walk a tightrope between opacity on the one hand and a sterile transparency on the other.

As to the sort of characterization of the practical arena which is desired, there are also two difficulties. We are not interested in reporting the immediately apparent details of this or that case of practical stancing, but in getting at the deep and generic. In regard to the first, we are not concerned with the mere show of surface phenomena, but with those structures which are disclosed as "counted on," "understood," present as a "structuring" of that show. These are, unlike colors, movements, and sounds, unarticulated at the level of immediate, qualitative imagery. (It is useful to recall the discussion in chapter 4 of the distinction between the datal and disclosive aspects of appearing; in getting at the structure of the practical arena, it is only the disclosive which is at issue.) Indeed, even our ordinary language of practice seems ill-suited to their depiction, directed, as it is, largely to the marking of diagnostically useful differences and similarities among things. Thus, in getting at the deep in our experience we often have to twist our language, putting it to a strain which diminishes our sense of familiarity. The device of metaphor is available, of course, and it cannot be altogether avoided, but survey seeks literal statement.

In regard to the generic, we have a similar difficulty. We are interested in reporting on the general structures, not the illustrative particularities. Yet our procedure cannot be one of straight-forward empirical generalization, for one may generalize only from particular data which have been particularized and indexed according to some manner of ordering which is either theoretical or practical, and the manner of the latter is part of what we may hope to elicit through survey by attention to the general. On the other hand, the very appearing of things as illustrative of the generic—a manner of appearing which was identified in chapter 4—cannot be taken at face value as the presentation of the genuinely general structures of the arena. The guises of things may sometimes be disguises. We are therefore caught between two inadequacies which, however, may serve in some measure to correct each other. The phenomenally generic provides a means of particularizing and selecting for generalization, but what is so phenomenally apparent is itself subject to reconsideration, even dismissal, on the basis of the success or lack of success of generalization. Of course, the major move for clarifying the phenomenally generic is, given a familiar domain, imaginative variation. But that is also the primary move of confirmation and disconfirmation. What results, then, is that neither the general nor the deep can simply be "read off" from the subject-matter by the surveyor; the possibilities of hasty conclusion and misdirected sentiment haunt one's every turn, and the recognition of their constant presence may even corrode one's confidence. Once more, an appreciation of these difficulties provides the best hope of melioration.

It would be nice if there were a proven method for getting us through all of these difficulties unscathed. If there were such a thing, we might want to call it a "phenomenological method." Unfortunately, there is no such thing. That which has historically gone under that title seems to me so thoroughly theoretically commissive as to encourage, usually with a great show of innocence, exactly the difficulties which we have discussed. The truth is that no approach or technique of survey of the non-theoretical can yield results which do not deserve suspicion. Let me emphasize this once and for all. One can only be forewarned against the pits and snares of survey and then proceed, with both perseverance and trepidation, to do the best he can.

2. So much for preliminaries. In the remainder of this chapter I will attempt to set out the structure of the practical arena as I think it may be elicited from the disclosures of practical stancing. I will do this in stages, beginning in this section with some preliminary observations regarding what I take to be essential to any characterization of the practical arena. In the next section I will consider an approach to the practical which is drawn from a different philosophical quarter, that of John Dewey, and I will attempt to show in what ways it confirms my own findings yet, to some extent, leads us astray. I then move, in the succeeding section, to the task of gathering these findings and certain additional points together into a general sketch. What is offered at this point is, however, less a unified structure than a set of structural components. I therefore conclude the chapter with a very tentative proposal regarding such a structure. At each of these stages I must go over many of the same points, but it is to be hoped that they will be seen in each succeeding context in a fresh light and not as mere repetitions to no furthering purpose.

I begin, then, by rehearsing and expanding a bit upon some of the remarks made in the first chapter regarding the practical situation.

What needs emphasis at the beginning is that the practical arena is an arena of action, a situation within which an agent acts and has his effect. The agent is thus a dynamic and transformative part of the situation itself, inseparable from it and interactive within it. As an interactive partner within the situation, the agent stands on all fours with the "things" that he encounters there. These things are not necessarily considered to be agents themselves, though some of them may be, but they are, like the stancing agent, efficacious in their own right, things with a resistance to his or her own efficacy. This very stubbornness of things provides the basis for their usability, for their manner of imposing their own way may be turned to alliance with the ways of the agent. This structure of agent-arena-thing constitutes the bedrock structure of practical life. It contrasts sharply with the subject-field-object structure of the theoretical stance.

It is useful to draw out this contrast of the theoretical with the practical, for, as we saw earlier, the stances involved, the terrains and inhabitants disclosed, and the commitments made in regard to what there is stand in stark opposition. The pivotal contrast, no doubt, is that, whereas the agent is in the midst of, efficacious among, and interactional with the things of his arena, the subject of the theoretical stance has no such position within the field which stands at the terminus of his consideration. The identification of the subject with an object within the field is therefore entirely illegitimate, and such "positing" of identity for the sake of getting on with theory is systematically undercut by the position of the "positer" outside the field as its subject. Thus, an agent who initiates the taking of the theoretical stance abdicates his position of being among things; withdrawing from the arena is the initial step for transforming it into a field of objects rather than an arena of things. But now we must remind ourselves that such withdrawal is unavoidably incomplete, since the agent may, by once again intruding, replace the field with an arena. No matter how desperately involved one may be in theoretical matters, the agent waits in the wings, ready at any moment to draw one back into the exigencies of practical life.

The sustaining of the theoretical has its rewards. There are fields of objects which subjecthood opens to one's gaze that cannot be intruded into as an agent, which is to say that the theoretical field is in some respects grander than the practical arena. Indeed, it can be extended indefinitely, thereby instituting frameworks of space, time, and logical status which are distinctively theoretical in nature. The farthest galaxies, the most distant past, the most tenuous abstractions become available to the subject as occupants of positions within a multiplicity of coordinate systems. The theoretical field has of its own nature no horizon. The practical arena, on the other hand, is always horizoned. There are practical limits to its status of being an arena, for it has no standing for the agent except in its coordination of efficacies in his life. But if the theoretical field is grand, it is also cramped. In its greatness it still offers no lodging for either the agent or the subject. The practical arena is, though limited, open; it allows the agent room to move, manipulate, make, dance. The theoretical field is, though always to some extent unexplored, determinate and filled. The objects that are found in space, time, and the abstractive matrix fill it; the theoretical field is a plenum of objects.

The openness of the arena is of another stripe than the extensity and unexplored unlimitedness of the field. Indeterminacy, emergence, surprise, and novelty in the field are always epistemic. In the arena of practical affairs they are substantive, axial. On the other hand, such theoretical notions and distinctions do not well characterize that openness. For the agent the arena is open to his action and its own transformation by virtue of it. This may incline us to say that the agent confronts something like possibilities. But the theoretical notion of a numerical diversity of possibilities, of possible future states of affairs, does not fit the agent's view of things. It is rather that the problematic situation and thus the arena as a whole is incomplete, unfinished. In such a view the doctrines of indeterminism and determinism simply have no meaningful application. The arena, in providing room for the agent to make and unmake, to move, to change, to get things done, is thus tolerant of alternative developments. The theoretical mind finds this way of putting things worse than untidy; it finds it scandalous. But from the practical stance this is the way of things, straightforwardly and hardheadedly.

The acceptance of agency carries with it persistence and habituation. The agent persists throughout his action, production, or transaction, and the things persist throughout that span of time over that terrain according to their natures. The notion of a succession of states of affairs, of the present as a frontier of actuality spawning events towards the future, is inapplicable within the practical stance. Things and the agent among them simply survive whatever changes occur, ensuring a stability in the future; passage occurs around them, among them, flows by them. The presence of persisting things is, practically speaking, prerequisite, for on the very integrity and self-determining efficacy of things rests the required stability for practical footing and the viability of manipulation. The practical conceptions of time and space derive from the importance of alteration, the span of action, the facts of coming to be and passing away, so that they need posit no homogeneous or abstract matrix in which things come to be. One doesn't exist first now and then later in a temporal dimension; he grows older, and age as a mark of survival and stability is respected. Time is something told, an instrument of practical moment. Space is something traveled and tallied, a device of agentival ordering; findable place and traversable distance are its desiderata; up and down, left and right, near and far, its dimensions. And the abstractive order is recognizable only as a distinction between doing and rehearsal; what the theoretical man calls abstractions—ideas, numbers, patterns, plans—are by the practical man construed as means of thinking one's way towards consummation.

The primacy of persisting things rather than that of states of affairs situated one after another within a general framework not only grounds the practical notions of time and space but establishes an order of habituation. Things persist according to their natures, but things of their sorts appear again. The success of practice demands the development of ways of recognizing and re-acting to the same sorts of things again and again. So it is that the practical stance relies upon a stability of sorts. Things being autonomous, efficacious on their own, precludes the notion of a merely conventional sorting of them. This idea, that sorting is a matter of adopting a classification on merely practical grounds and thus that classification is merely relative to interest, is a theoretical explanation of why practical men sort the way they do. It is a theory and perhaps a useful one. But at the level of the practical stance this view is absurd. There, the idea is to take account of things by learning to see them as they are, i.e., as resistances, centers of efficacy, in the arena. They are of the sorts they are naturally, i.e., by virtue of what they are on their own. If we once reconstruct the practical arena as a field of objects which are, on their own, inefficacious, unresisting, non-interactional, then we will of course wonder on what basis they might be ordered in practice. We could only assume that their practical grouping must be relative to some prescient practical aiming. Blind things cannot find their own niches. But once one sees that the practical arena is interactional, that things are partners on an equal footing with the agent, it becomes easy to see that they are not blind, but demanding of their own places in our despite.

3. The picture of the practical arena which is emerging is, as one might expect, similar in many respects to the characterization of experience which one often finds in the works of those philosophers who, above all others, have paid the practical a proper respect, namely, the American Pragmatists. This resemblance is especially striking in regard to John Dewey's depiction of what he has on occasion referred to as "primary experience." But it would appear that Dewey's project is a little different from mine both in its emphasis and in its target and, though our results are often complementary, it will be illuminating in regard to my own project to note these differences.

In *Experience and Nature,* Dewey introduces the distinction between primary and secondary (or derived) experience in this way:

> This consideration of method may suitably begin with the contrast between gross, macroscopic, crude subject-matters in primary experience and the refined, derived objects of reflection. The distinction is one between what is experienced as the result of a minimum of incidental reflection and what is experienced in

consequence of continued and regulated reflective inquiry. For derived and refined products are experienced only because of the intervention of systematic thinking. The objects of both science and philosophy obviously belong chiefly to the secondary and re-fined system . . .

. . . That the subject-matter of primary experience sets the prob-lems and furnishes the first data of the reflection which constructs the secondary objects is evident; it is also obvious that test and verification of the latter is secured only by return to things of crude or macroscopic experience—the sun, earth, plants, and an-imals of common, every-day life. . . . They *explain* the primary objects, they enable us to grasp them with *understanding*. . . . (15–16)

Now, two things about this approach stand out in contrast with my con-cern with the practical arena, namely, its methodological focus and its in-attention to the diversity of stancing. Let me expand a bit on each.

It is clear that Dewey's concern in making the distinction is methodo-logical; it focuses, as do almost all of Dewey's discussions of experience throughout his writings, on the consideration of what is relevant to pro-viding a proper understanding of reflective inquiry. This is to say that his interest in primary experience and his depiction of it is less concerned with being true to how it appears in its own right—as is my concern at this point—than it is with its initiating, evidential, and verifying roles in the transformative process of inquiry. It is hardly to be expected, then, that this difference of emphasis, of selective interest, would lead to pre-cisely the same characterization of a shared subject-matter. In particular, my interest is in how the components of the subject-matter stand out and are involved or interrelated with each other in and as constituting their own context, whereas Dewey's is invariably that of construing these com-ponents and interrelations as they stand in the context of inquiry. Differ-ence in context yields, as Dewey was always at pains to remind us, differ-ences in what is taken to be important and, consequently, in how things are characterized.

Moreover, the actual subject-matter to be characterized seems to be different. I am concerned with that which is disclosed within one specific stance among others, whether that involve a reflective component or not; Dewey is concerned with prereflective experience at large without spec-ification as relative to stance. One way of putting this is to say that Dew-ey's distinction between primary and derivative experience is itself differ-ent from and perhaps even cuts across the distinction which I wish to make between stances and their disclosures. What serves to blur this difference is the great similarity between Dewey's characterization of primary experience and the characterization which I have, at least so far, given of the practical arena. This is a fact which cries out for explanation. From my side, I would tend to explain it like this. Dewey is actually attempting to provide a picture of everyday life in its prereflective presence and, since practical stancing has primacy and centricity in all of life, that picture will be, if at all adequate, responsive to this primacy. From Dewey's side the explanation might be that, though he does not (here or elsewhere in his writings) attend to the compelling fact of the diversity of stancing in our lives, he nonetheless assumes something *like* the primacy of practical stancing, namely, the primacy of the concerns and ends of the agent of practical affairs. In any case, the fact is that, though Dewey's subject-matter of primary experience may not exactly coincide with that of the practical arena, it overlaps with it to a significant extent.

There are two ways in which Dewey may appear, at least at first glance, to be attentive to the diversity of stancing. The first is that he often does make a point of contrasting "common sense inquiry," as he calls it, and scientific inquiry in such a way as to suggest a distinction of practical and theoretical stancing. The way in which he characterizes each suggests a distinction among the types of inquiry which are engaged upon from within the two stances. This suggestion is, however, undermined to the extent that he presents scientific inquiry as itself essentially practical, transformative, and agentive. Nonetheless, when his concern is to characterize everyday deliberation, the closeness to practical stancing as such is compelling. In the following passage from his *Logic* this closeness is obvious, though, as typical, his characterization of the "deliberative arena," as we might call it, is selectively focused upon what he wishes to indicate as its methodologically or, as he refers to it here, its "logically" relevant features.

> By description, the situations which *evoke* deliberation resulting in decision, are themselves indeterminate with respect to what might and should be done. They require that *something* should be done. But *what* action is to be taken is just the thing in question. The problem of *how* the uncertain situation should be dealt with is urgent. But as merely urgent, it is so emotional as to impede and often to frustrate wise decision. The intellectual question is what sort of action the *situation* demands in order that it may receive a satisfactory objective reconstruction . . .
> . . . I shall summarize formally what is logically involved in every situation of deliberation and grounded decision in matters of practice. There is an existential situation such that (a) its constitu-

ents are changing so that in any case *something* different is going to happen in the future; and such that (b) just *what* will exist in the future depends in part upon introduction of *other* existential conditions interacting with those already existing, while (c) *what* new conditions are brought to bear depends upon what activities are undertaken, (d) the latter matter being influenced by the intervention of inquiry in the way of observation, inference and reasoning. (163–64)

The second way in which a sensitivity to stancing may be thought to be revealed in Dewey's writings is in regard to his concerted attack upon the assumption, which he takes to be endemic to traditional philosophy, of the epistemic and metaphysical priority of a removed and external or "spectator's" point of view. To my knowledge, however, he never identifies this point of view with what I have called theoretical stancing, and perhaps he shouldn't, for it is not so much the manner of viewing things which he finds at fault (after all, he does seem to want to provide it with an important place in "scientific" inquiry), as it is a certain assumption made about how its objects are to be understood. (I would, of course, understand this assumption, not as something externally imposed on this manner of viewing things by the philosophical tradition, but as native to it by virtue of its constitutive reality-claim; its adoption is therefore unsurprising if not altogether forgivable, because it represents an assumption which theoretically engaged philosophers would find insistently present in their work.) Dewey's criticism of this "point of view" is that, besides resulting in philosophical dualisms and other dead-ends, it involves an unjustified denigration of the practical dimension of everyday life. On occasion, as in the 1908 article "Does Reality Possess Practical Character?", he goes so far as to speak in behalf of an affirmative answer to that question. But we should not conclude that he understands this position to represent or include a reality-claim which is native to a certain manner of stancing. He never indicates in so many words that he is concerned with stancing at all.

These differences in regard to what I am up to in this chapter and what Dewey is doing have consequences for the language which we may allow ourselves to employ in the characterization of our subject-matters. Dewey tends to introduce into his depiction of primary experience a certain terminology which is derived, not from what appears as it appears at that level, but from certain biological accounts of it. Thus, his predilection to speak of it as structured into organism and environment, which is denied to one who attempts to characterize the practical arena in pretheoretic and nonsystemic terms, may be forgiven when it is understood that his way of putting things is taken by him to have methodological value and that, in our present philosophical lives taken as inclusive of certain theoretical influences, such terms are common coin. Such anomalous language aside, the points of similarity between his usual characterization of his subject-matter and my characterization of mine are telling. Consider, for example, these remarks from his justly famous 1917 essay "The Need for a Recovery of Philosophy."

> The experience of a living being struggling to hold its own and make its way in an environment, physical and social, partly facilitating and partly obstructing its actions, is of necessity a matter of ties and connections, of bearings and uses. The very point of experience, so to say, is that it doesn't occur in a vacuum; its agent-patient instead of being insulated and disconnected is bound up with the movement of things by most intimate and pervasive bonds. Only because the organism is in and of the world, and its activities correlated with those of other things in multiple ways, is it susceptible to undergoing things and capable of trying to reduce objects to means of securing its good fortune. That these connections are of diverse kinds is irresistibly proved by the fluctuations which occur in its career. Help and hindrance, stimulation and inhibition, success and failure mean specifically different modes of correlation. Although the actions of things in the world are taking place in one continuous stretch of existence, there are all kinds of specific affinities, repulsions, and relative indifferencies. (11)

In this passage the phrases 'in and of the world' and 'things in the world' deserve comment. Though in the larger ambit of our ordinary lives we may see ourselves and things as being "in the world," this can hardly be taken as the gift of practical stancing *per se,* for both the agent and the things disclosed within such stancing appear as *situated,* not in a single and encompassing world, but in a localized and horizoned *terrain.* The difference between being in a situation and being in a world is, I would say, so fundamental that it is a primary responsibility of philosophers to avoid confusing them at all costs. They represent incorrigibly different senses of 'being in'. The fact that Dewey slips into this reference to a world may perhaps be taken as additional confirmation of our conclusion that his subject-matter is different from our own.[14]

The notion of connection which is introduced in this passage was central to Dewey's view of experience throughout his career. That this is to be understood in terms of the varieties and degrees of influence is emphasized in remarks which follow that passage.

Some things are relatively insulated from the influence of other things; some things are easily invaded by others; some things are fiercely attracted to conjoin their activities with those of others. Experience exhibits every kind of connection from the most intimate to mere external juxtaposition. (11–12)

An interesting footnote to these remarks is appended.

> The word relation suffers from ambiguity. I am speaking here of *connexion,* dynamic and functional interaction. "Relation" is a term used to express logical reference. I suspect that much of the controversy about internal and external relations is due to this ambiguity. One passes at will from existential connections of things to logical relationship of terms. Such an identification of existences with *terms* is congenial to idealism, but is paradoxical in a professed realism. (12)

This expansion upon the use of 'connection' as "dynamic and functional interaction" is a bit confusing. There is a bare suggestion here that the things of experience appear, not autonomously and integrally, but as functions of the interaction itself, whereas the reference to things as being in some cases "relatively insulated from the influence of other things" and the reference to connection as being in some cases "mere external juxtaposition" would seem to indicate otherwise. I draw attention to this because in Dewey's subsequent publications, as he became more and more aware of this ambiguity, he drifted towards the more functional interpretation. Indeed, he came to favor the term 'transaction' over 'interaction' as better indicating what he came to take as the more concrete fact of a process from which specific things may be selectively abstracted for certain purposes. This is unfortunate for our purposes, however, for the brute fact is that in the practical arena the things, or at least many of them, appear as having the status of individuals which resist some influences as surely as they welcome others. The term 'interaction' is therefore more appropriate to the practical arena as it is disclosed. Dewey's eventual replacement of it represents, I believe, the invasion of his "phenomenology," so to speak, by a theoretical attachment, hardly to be despised on its own merits, to a process metaphysics.

Dewey provides something like an argument for his view of experience as involving connections in the immediately succeeding passage of this article.

> Empirically, then, active bonds of continuities of all kinds, together with static discontinuities, characterize existence. To deny

> this qualitative heterogeneity is to reduce the struggles and diffi-
> culties of life, its comedies and tragedies, to illusion: to the non-
> being of the Greeks or to its modern counterpart, the "subjective."
> Experience is an affair of facilitations and checks, of being sus-
> tained and disrupted, being let alone, being helped and troubled,
> of good fortune and defeat in all the countless qualitative modes
> which these words pallidly suggest. The existence of genuine con-
> nections of all manner of heterogeneity cannot be doubted. Such
> words as conjoining, disjoining, resisting, modifying, saltatory, and
> ambulatory (to use James's picturesque term) only hint at their ac-
> tual heterogeneity. (12)

The point seems to be that experience of this sort is inextricably embedded in our lives and that to deny its apparent authenticity in respect to
"existence" is therefore to make of our lives something it cannot be
taken to be, namely, a grand illusion. If this is what is involved here, it is
similar to an argument which I presented in the previous chapter. It is, to
say the least, ontological in import.

Let me close this consideration of Dewey's survey of everyday experience in the large, so to speak, by bemoaning the fact that, though he may
well have carried it further and deeper than those who philosophized
before him, he did not push it as far as he might have. For one of the
most compelling facts about our everyday life is that it admits of diverse
manners of experiencing and orienting ourselves to things and that each
of these manners carries with its taking an assumption, incorrigible
within it, in regard to what is real and authentic. And, if I am right, that
deserves a focus upon practical stancing which Dewey may have approached but in fact never quite achieved.

4. Thus far my observations regarding the practical arena have been
scattered and fragmentary. Let me now attempt to gather them together
into a more cohesive picture. In doing so, I shall introduce (in italics) a
certain terminology which is to some degree fixed and technical, though
not, I hope, reflective of any specific systemic ordering or regimentation.

The practical arena presents itself as *changing* in some respects while
enduring in others, *unstable* in some respects while *stable* in others, but
in any case *unfinished* towards the future as it is *finished* towards the
past. To pause a moment here, the verbal character of these distinctions is significant. The scope of practical interest is not a field of changes,
but an arena in which things and situations are changing. It is not that
states earlier and later which are characterized by some property of identity across time are then taken as things, but that things, being what they

are, endure, maintain themselves by virtue of the integrity of their inherent power, "on their own steam" as it were. Their persistence be-
speaks their craft at survival, often in spite of superficial changing and
reshaping. Their failure to persist marks their lack of self-determination,
their weakness, their susceptibility to the forces of others. Is it surprising that courage and self-reliance, as well as craft and adaptability, become the virtues of the agents who inhabit the arena? It is also significant
that these distinctions—changing/enduring, unstable/stable, unfinished/
finished—do not cut along the same lines. There is stability in the manner of changing, and the enduring thing may outlive its proper span,
thereby destabilizing the present situation. Moreover, the present situation, unfinished towards the future is at the same time finished towards
the past. The past, set and immovable, intrudes into the present, though
never so as to fix that present unalterably, to leave no room for intervention. There is, then, no knife-edge present, no dimensionless instant, in
the practical arena. Its span is marked by the scope of conduct, by the
shape of project. The notion of change as the contrast of two instanta-
neous states of affairs is theoretical. Practically, changing takes time or,
to put it more properly, changing determines time, both as a span and
direction.

To these structural correlates should be added those of *focus/back-
ground/horizon* and *option/avenue*. From the standpoint of the agent,
there is a focal area of indeterminacy, the situation, which is surrounded
and supported, temporally, spatially, and habitually, by a background of
the determinate. Orientation is provided by this background, by one's
sense of left and right, one's reliable skills and habits, the dependability
of tools and landmarks, the settled "facts" of the past. As a background it
is far or near, and it recedes from the agent's grasp towards a horizon
which marks the limit of the arena. Like the horizon where earth and sky
meet, this boundary encloses the arena from a here which determines it.
The things of the background, however, mark a landscape of their own,
for each of them, there, institutes a here which it determines by its own
place. Thus, the agent is able, in recognizing the thing as something on
its own, to take the place of the other, to see it as having its own surroundings, near to horizoned far. In this way the agent can "take account" of things in their own right, anticipate their manners of tractability
or resistance, provide them with roles in his ongoing projects. With such
understanding the agent confronts his own surroundings of things, not as
a deterrent to his own action, but as an arena of alternatives, as an opening of avenues which may be taken upon his own option. Such avenues
among things and options by the agent are not seen as separable, as possibilities in nature and choices available to the agent, but as existing in

an integral unity of alternativeness. The option taken is the avenue taken, and no dichotomization of the sort often theoretically proposed is apparent. The notion that there are possibilities which I could take were I not determined to the choice I make is practically inexpressible.

The mix of instability and stability, together with the presence of agentive option, determine the arena to be, always, a place of both *risk* and *fortune* and thus, insistently, of *lures* which each avenue of action offers of itself in some degree. The arena is not a mute or passive situation of openings, but beckons, calls out to the agent in many voices and with many offerings. But the threat of failure also haunts the avenues, so that any path taken is imbued with jeopardy, an aura of the intractable waywardness of things, and a penumbra of an insurmountable residue of blind luck, whatever one's skill and familiarity with things and however careful one may be.

The agent, many things, and the focus of problematic concern present themselves as movable, as allowing that the landscape may, within limits to be discovered, traversed, and that the horizon may "recede" in the direction of movement. Thus, the agent moves about, carrying his focus with him, so to speak, so long as he remains practically stanced. However differently a traversed landscape may appear to be, it is understood to be uniformly available as an arena, to be *ubiquitously arenaed.* This is to say that no foundational regionalization or stratification of things and situations is provided by the practical arena as such, but, if present in one's practical life, an addition, an enrichment. It is also to say that the practical arena is not disclosed as one specifiable terrain, one problematic focus, within one determinate landscape of things or one ultimate and encompassing horizon. To gather its localized cases into one world, one whole, would require a point of view beyond its own. We might put these observations in terms external and alien to the ambit of disclosure by saying that the practical arena as such is neither regionalized nor encompassed by a world. Speaking from within, we might say that the arena is intransigently *localizing* yet *traversable* and hence alternatively *localizable.*

Finally, the status of agent and thing requires specification. Each is *ensconced* within the arena by virtue of its *interactional involvement* with the others. Yet each is also, within limits, *autonomous*—efficacious, resistant, unremitting to the degree of its own integrity. Moreover, each is of a distinctive *natural sort* by virtue of that same integrity, by virtue of what it is on its own. Agents are radically different in kind from things which are not agents, but nonagents are also naturally sortable. And all such natural sorts, though recognizable by the agent by means of his habituation to their manners of appearance, are nonetheless understood to be determined, not by appearances, but by the "natures" of their occupants, i.e., by virtue of what the things of that sort are on their own as autonomous beings. The division among sorts, together with the manners of efficacy, enduring, and changing which are native to their occupants, lay the very foundations of whatever order and stability may be found within the arena. Instability occurs within these foundations and among their ruins, in the present and at the focus of indeterminacy, as, for whatever reason, the agent attends to the unfinished and open nature of his situation.

5. In this sketch of the practical arena I have tried to identify those components of it which are structurally constitutive, but how they come together into a single, unified structure is not yet altogether obvious. I will now make some suggestions about this. This attempt puts us on the edge of theory, of providing an *account* of that limited subject-matter which has been labeled "the practical arena." But we may not step across this border and into theory, even though what is proposed must be taken to be, as a proposal, hypothetical and subject to critical evaluation. What is to be avoided is, first of all, the sort of terminological shift which comes with theoretical sharpening, idealization, and regimentation and, second, the imposition of a form of structuring which is derived from systemic and otherwise theoretic commitments. I must attempt, therefore, both (i) to be faithful to the pretheoretic language which I have already employed, extending it, if I find it useful to do so, only in such a way as to allow for full explication in its terms, and (ii) to extricate the deep and generic structure from the presented phenomena, the stance-bound disclosures, themselves. With these things in mind, I propose the following.

In conformity with our earlier conclusion that a structure consists, minimally, of the specification of both basic sorts of entities and certain means for ordering them, the structure of the practical arena may be said to have the general form of the specification of (a) two basic sorts of entities: *individuals* and *arena*, (b) a basic limiting order on the arena provided by *natural sorts* of individuals, and (c) two basic modes of specifying order in respect to the arena: individual-to-individual *involvements* and arena-to-individual *centering*. Individuals will be said to be *structurally primary*. They have, that is, *structural primacy over* all other items, i.e., over the arena itself, their own natural sorts, and the involvements and centering which order the arena. By saying that something of sort A has structural primacy over something of sort B, I mean to indicate that, within the context of the relevant subject-matter, the presence of any specific B is disclosed as being "grounded in" and "dependent on" the presence of some As, and not vice versa.

The minimal structure offered has the seductive appearance of coherence. One wants coherence in an ontological system, of course, and that is what tends to seduce us, but the structural picture of the practical arena which we must be satisfied with is one which is true to what is disclosed, whether it be coherent or not. In the above picture the apparently coherence-inducing element is clearly the principle of the structural primacy of individuals. To the extent that it is taken as such, it must be looked upon with a healthy suspicion. I have not, however, introduced it uncritically; it seems to me to be fully justified by the subject-matter to which it has been applied, though only in the rather vague form in which it has in fact been formulated. I have tried, in fact, to formulate the notion of structural primacy in such a way as to avoid the certification of coherence while yet leaving that possibility open. As a result, the notions of "grounding" and "dependence" which have been employed must remain intuitive at this level, unregimented by appeal to theory, and yet capable of illustration by appeal to the disclosures of the subject-matter. It is a consequence of this, however, that they can only be taken as lacking the precision and systemic fixity which would seem to be necessary for theoretic use. This is the way it has to be. But it illustrates part of a broader problem which will be discussed in the next chapter.[15]

I will now attempt to clarify what is involved in this structure.

To include the arena as an entity of a distinct sort from that of individuals is to indicate that it is a unity and not a mere multiplicity of individuals. Each arena is in fact an entity constituted by individuals which determine, by virtue of their involvements with one another and their roles in centering, the specific order of that arena. Thus, as regards the basic entities, individuals are structurally primary.[16]

It will be noted that in the above statement of the general structure of the practical arena, I have replaced the innocuous term 'thing', which I have heretofore employed for the inhabitants of the arena, with the term 'individual'. I have done this in order to emphasize a point of substance about "things," namely, that each is effective on its own and in virtue of what it is on its own. This is to say that each such thing is of the natural sort it is and enters into the involvements it does by virtue, not of what it is in general, but of what it is in its own numerically unique individuality. An arena does not have this character, for though it can be said to be something on its own, it does not, as a single entity, enter into any involvement with anything. This was indicated under (c) by the qualification on involvements as being "individual to individual." Nor, it should be said, are there natural sorts of arenas, at least on the structure proposed, as was indicated under (b).

The structural primacy of individuals over natural sorts rests on the principle that each individual is determined to be of the natural sort it is by its being the individual it is on its own and not, therefore, by its standing in a certain role or involvement imposed upon it by anything else. The structural primacy of individuals over involvements is both specific as regards those involvements and general as regards their varieties. Thus, (1) individuals determine, in their togetherness but by virtue of what each is in its own integrity, the *specific* involvements in which they stand and (2) each individual establishes, by virtue of the natural sort which it is of, the *general* ways in which it may be involved with other individuals.

It is by virtue of (2) that the "limiting order" of component (b) of the proposed structure is made available. The order is to be understood as providing a general limitation on the involvements of individuals and, by extension, on the roles, central or otherwise, of those individuals in an arena. As an arena-wide mode of ordering, it is taxonomic; it provides something like a hierarchical schema of natural sorts, from natural genera to natural species, in terms of which constraints and allowances upon how individuals may, in general, be together can be made out. What must not be forgotten, however, is that this taxonomic order is not only limiting on the specific individuals of a specific arena, but it is an ordering which is imposed by those individuals. The point is important. The order is not preset and imposed on those individuals from without or antecedently. Thus, every schema of such ordering which may be carried forward by an agent from one situation to another must remain open to the recognition of natural sorts which those individuals which appear in the new situation present to the agent in their own behalf and in his own despite.

It is assumed on this structural proposal that the actual web of involvement among individuals serves to determine the arena to be the specific arena it is. What this comes to is perhaps obvious on its face. What may not be so obvious, however, is the manner in which, as indicated under (c), these actual involvements exhibit a specifying order *in respect to the arena*. The general point is easily made. A structural order which is disclosed in any practical arena cannot consist of the *de facto* specifics of this or that arena, so, if there is to be a structural ordering observed by the specifics of involvement among specific individuals, that ordering could only be exhibited by their generic character. On the other hand, we must allow an indefinitely extensive range of varieties of involvements, for we must allow the individuals to express themselves in their own and perhaps novel, even surprising, ways. These two facts together suggest that the many diverse sorts of involvements nonetheless impose on the arena certain specifiable *dimensions,* as I will call them, of the organization of involvements. I will return to the consideration of what such dimensions might be disclosed to be in a moment.

First, however, we need to distinguish such dimensions of *involvements* from the order of roles of *individuals* which is also grounded in and dependent on specific involvements. What I have in mind by this reference to roles is that positioning of individuals about a central figure, the stancing agent. This positioning is such as to structure the arena in a horizoned and localizing fashion. That this structuring is dependent on the web of involvement itself is clear from the fact that the arena diminishes in the strength and influence of its involvements with any individual agent within it to a vanishing point of a total lack of disclosed relevance for the purposes of the action of that agent. The structural primacy of involvement over centering comes to that. But the fact that the arena is always uniquely centered is not itself grounded on this basis alone. What is additionally involved can be stated, even though its intelligibility (which it is not our present task to supply) is difficult to make out. We can only say this much. That a certain individual *a* stands in the central role in an arena depends on three factors, namely, that the role is allowed it by other individuals *bcd* . . . which are involved with *a* to such a degree as to be brought within *a*'s ambit of involvement, that *a* is itself of a natural sort which is capable of occupying that role (i.e., is an agent capable of standing among those other individuals and in a web of involvement with them), and that *a* in fact occupies that role. As to actual occupation, it may, at the one extreme, be resisted by an individual which can and is allowed to assume it or, at the other extreme, be forced upon such an individual by others. There is no doubt that, theoretically considered, this fact of unique centering is mysterious, if not altogether opaque, but it remains a fact that this is how the matter is disclosed within practical stancing. To take this fact as altogether illusory would be to take the practical arena as illusory.

What has thus far emerged is little more than a clarification of the very general structure which was introduced at the beginning of this section. Further specification regarding the taxonomy of the limiting order and dimensions of the specifying order of involvements cannot be altogether avoided by the investigator, however, for certain further divisions within these modes of order would appear to be constitutive of any practical arena. I feel compelled, then, to elaborate a bit on them, even though I find myself less confident about the divisions proposed than about the fact that some such divisions are called for.

I suggest as the basic genera of individuals those of the cohesively focused and nonfocused (i.e., something like that which is reflected in ordinary language as sortals and mass terms), and I propose as a further division among focused individuals a split betwen agents and nonagents. Providing these divisions with a further yet pretheoretic explication is a delicate business and one I shall forego. A closer understanding may be gained through the consideration of the further subsorts of each, but I shall not pursue the matter here.

What I have in mind by ordering dimensions of involvement is that all individuals involve themselves with others so as to institute, in their togetherness, more or less separable manners of construing their arrangement. An analogue in eighteenth-century thought is available for this, consisting of the alternative arrangements of things in their "causal" interrelations, their spatial and temporal placement, and their apparent fittingness and lack of fittingness in regard to each other. It seems to me that these proposed dimensions of order, considered apart from the peculiarly provincial understanding of the natures of entities and the specific sorts of relations sustained among them which was fashionable at that time, reflect an ordinary and everyday view of things which is rooted in practical affairs. In any case, I propose as the four dimensions of order of the involvements in a practical arena what I shall call the *dynamic,* the *spatial,* the *temporal,* and the *proprietive.* In distinguishing them in this way, I recognize that I am running the risk of giving the impression that each of them rests upon a distinctive and separable set of involvements. This is not at all my intention, for it seems more likely to me that every manner or variety of involvement contributes to more than one (and possibly to all) of these dimensional orders. Now let me say something briefly about each.

Of these dimensions, the one which tends to be most often theoretically slighted is the proprietive, but for practical stancing of any variety it is a brute fact. The arena offers itself to the stancing agent as avenued, open, luring, risky, and a place of gain, loss, good fortune, and defeat. The deepening of this dimension in the moral species of practical stancing is obvious. And it goes without saying that what is most distant, spatially or temporally, or less influencing or capable of being influenced tends to be seen as less proprietively relevant, demanding, or luring. And vice versa.

The application of the dynamic to what appears is often questioned on certain theoretical grounds as well, for from the theoretical stance and on certain theoretic assumptions about its field of objects, the objects do not serve to produce or influence anything on their own, but are taken to exemplify a "law" of succession or functional variation which only indicates how they are found to be associated with one another and, perhaps, the operation of some genuine "causal" force behind the scenes. But within practical stancing what is straightforwardly disclosed are things which impose themselves on others in various ways, which persist, fade, grow, and decrease in force and influence; they are disclosed, not merely as things which can be taken as signs, but as pointing, tending, acting towards and from. We have seen Dewey make this point forcefully in regard to what he calls "connections."

The presence of the spatial and temporal dimensions seems quite obvious. The important facts about them are that they are to be understood in practical terms and that they are determined in *their* dimensions by the individuals which are disclosed as having a place within them. Thus, neither dimension is disclosed as an antecedently given medium in which individuals are placed and spread their influence, but in terms of intervals which mark the span of action and traversal and in terms of directions and locations which indicate and are indicated by pathways, avenues, spheres of influence, change, and the opening and closing of the arena. The point is often made, and properly, that space and time are differently understood aesthetically, theoretically, mythically, and—what is significant here—practically.

A final point about the structure proposed in this section might be made. It is typical of philosophers to think of a structure as necessarily involving entities of a sort which are dependent on others in a special way, namely, as properties, attributes, relations, or—to make the point in a typically systemic way—functions of those others considered as particulars. This is of course a highly refined theoretical prejudice. In any case, nothing like these sorts of dependent entities has been elicited here. The reason for this is not that it is not proper to speak of individuals as having aspects or being characterizable in some way or other, but that these aspects or features represent, always, the ways individuals stand towards other individuals and are therefore part and parcel of their power and influence. Facing another, an individual presents a face to that other indeed, but the face it offers is part of what it is up to, of how it imposes its influence on others. On the other side, the face which one individual grasps from another is part of what that grasping individual is up to, an expression of its own manner of influencing or being influenced by others. What comes out of this is a mutual adjustment of individuals and, thus, a single, seamless fact of involvement. That an involvement of two individuals, considered of course in abstraction from the web of involvements among all of the individuals in the arena, is disclosed as both one thing and yet two-faced in this way is clear enough; that it appears as something which is more or less superficially disclosable, i.e., both as a surface show of that which may well represent the duplicities and guises of each individual and as a yet deeper confrontation each to each which appears through that surface and "throbbing underneath it" (Ortega y Gasset, *MQ* 62), is also clear. But that neither this horizontal sidedness nor this vertical polarity, as we might call them, is disclosed as either the product of the conjoining of distinguishable parts or the gift of a complexity of such elements as particulars, relations, and properties is hardly any less patent.

7

The Ontological
Availability of the Practical

◆◆◆   1. We begin all of our theoretical investigations upon consid-
        eration of and concern for what comes to pass, in some man-
ner or other, within our lives. Ontology, which purports to be an investigation of reality, can be no exception to this. The mere fact of such
concern is not enough, however, to ensure the legitimacy of such an
investigation. What must be established for that purpose is not merely
that the concern and consequent questioning which it motivates have a
genuine basis in our lives, but that, at a minimum, both the subject-
matter to which the questioning is directed and the theoretical objective
of that questioning can be identified and embraced by different investiga-
tors. If these conditions are satisfied by ontological investigation—and I
have argued in chapters 1 to 3 that they are—we can conclude that it is
at least an intelligible and meaningful concern.

But one is quite right, I think, to feel that the legitimization of ontological investigation must provide more than firm footing in respect to its
two poles of initiation and end; it should provide as well some reasonable footing for the process of investigation itself, for proceeding from
the one pole and towards the other. For that, I have argued, there is
needed some access to its subject-matter which can serve both to guide

the inquiry and to offer some promise of providing evidence relevant to the evaluation of hypotheses which may be proposed at any of its stages. I have also argued, however, that a grand appeal to life in its fullness is quite unhelpful as such an access, for though adequacy to the totality of the ingredients of our lives would satisfy a crucial condition for adjudication among rival ontological systems which are thought to be more or less complete, such "evidence of adequation" is simply incapable of providing incremental and limiting control within the course of inquiry itself. It seems, then, that what is needed in order to ensure the legitimacy of the process of ontological inquiry is the specification of a limited domain of evidence which deserves to be accorded favored status by the inquirer. Such a domain of evidence could only be located, however, by the identification of a favored manner of access to reality which is present within the life of any ontological questioner. Given the identification of such favored access, ontological inquiry may be taken to have achieved legitimacy as a manner of inquiring into its subject-matter. It is not only meaningful in regard to its questioning and its end, but tenable as a process of pursuing such questioning and proceeding incrementally towards the achievement of that end. It follows from this that, given my argument for the identification of practical stancing as favored access in chapter 5, my argument in support of the legitimacy of the ontological enterprise is complete.

This tenability is tenuous. It does not, of itself, enable one to proceed with any sure-footedness upon the course of inquiry. It is not sufficient to provide for the viability, as I have called it, of ontology. For this, we need more than a mere indication of where the appropriate evidence may be found, even more than the recognition that we are committed to the task of attempting to gather it there; we need to be able to gather it, to make it available for ontological use, and thus to articulate it in such a way as to be acceptable to and serviceable for each ontological inquirer. Indeed, no investigation can be said to be viable unless the process of proceeding towards its goal is subject to the directive controls of an available evidence which anyone who engages upon it is constrained to accept. Failing this, an enterprise, however legitimate it may be taken to be, is subject to the criticism that it offers no genuine promise of ever getting us anywhere. It would be as though, yearning desperately to find our way towards light, we were yet eternally doomed to grope and stumble in the dark.

Of course, viability is not conditioned by the possibility of terminal victory. A manner of theoretical investigation is terminable, let us say, only if its goal, its ideal of satisfactory theory, is in principle achievable. Francis Bacon apparently thought that science was terminable—we could gain the whole truth and the full truth in time. Today we find this a bit hard to swallow. The process of moving towards that goal is, we tend to think, viable, but the consummation of that process in an achievement of completely adequate scientific knowledge is, we also tend to think, unreachable even in principle. We do not think less of the scientific enterprise for all that. And I think we should say the same for ontology; nonterminable it may be, but we have no right to dismiss it on that ground alone. If it is viable as a manner of inquiry, that will be enough, I should think, for any philosopher.

Success in determining the exact point at which viability is achieved is, in an investigation as in fetal development, elusive. It is perhaps best, then, to consider viability as a matter of degree. I will argue in a moment that each succeeding stage of analysis which was proposed in the previous chapter would, if found acceptable, support a greater degree of viability for the ontological enterprise. Unfortunately, I have—and I think anyone should have—less confidence in the prospects at each stage than in the one which went before. Part of the basis for such diminishing returns is due to the fact that what may be proposed at each stage presupposes the results of the prior stage. But part of it is due to the limiting character of the project itself and cannot be overcome merely by succeeding at it. I will close my discussion in this chapter and this book with an attempt to show why this is so and how one might proceed, by moving to another plane of analysis, to overcome this limitation.

2. What is at issue in regard to viability is the availability of the right sort of evidence for the purpose of providing directive control on the course of ontological construction. The right sort of evidence, I have maintained, must, first of all, represent in some significant manner the structure of the practical arena. For this, it must be, in the second place, such as to be garnerable, elicitable, by any ontological questioner. Now, what is so elicited provides initially only what might be called the raw or first-level evidence. This is not to say that it does not represent genuine evidence nor that it is of no use at all in forwarding inquiry. But it is to say, in the third place, that its articulation for the purpose of providing a structure to which a hypothesis may be fitted or compared for fit requires a certain care and precision in its representation. The first-level evidence, that is, must be prepared in anticipation of theoretic service. Whatever might result from such preparation would therefore be a sort of evidence which is less raw and more refined than that at the original level, a sort of second-level evidence which is proposed as mediating between purely pretheoretic and focally theoretic concerns.

Ideally, of course, such second-level evidence would remain *com-*

pletely faithful to the first-level evidence as it is disclosed and yet be, at the same time, *thoroughly* satisfying to demands which derive from another and quite different quarter. That the achievement of this ideal would be a delicate and difficult matter goes without saying. I am, in fact, skeptical of its very possibility. But it does not seem to me, in any case, that such ideal achievement should be taken as required for viability. It is, I would say, no more than an ideal of a manner of inquiry which has already shown itself to be viable. A viable inquiry will, no doubt, posit such an ideal and it may well be judged as more or less promising in the pursuit of its goal to the extent that it approximates that ideal, but it seems to me to be asking too much of any inquiry which has its roots in everyday affairs to demand such perfection of it.

The fact remains that the ontological inquirer cannot rest satisfied with first-level evidence alone. The extent to which such evidence is found to be achievable will, indeed, surely show as well that some degree of the viability of the enterprise may be assumed. But only to the extent that second-level evidence is shown to be available can it be assumed that the enterprise is viable to any very high or satisfying degree. The precise degree of viability which one *should* find satisfying does not, I think, admit of impartial determination, but something significantly higher than that guaranteed on the basis of first-level evidence would seem to be a reasonable expectation.

3. Clearly, the weight of making a case for viability falls to chapter 6, for, in the end, the only way of showing that the proper sort of evidence *can* be made available is to carry one through a process which *does in fact* result in the presentation of some acceptable cases of it. But it must be clear by now that the purported evidence presented in that chapter was always strained, either in the direction of the pull of faithfulness to the pretheoretic disclosures or in the direction of the pull of availability for theoretical control. The process of presentation was, in fact, incremental, moving from the favoring of the first pull to the favoring of the second.

Three phases in this presentation of evidence may be identified. They may be restated in the terms introduced in the last section as follows: (a) the identification of first-level evidence consisting of various structural elements of the practical arena which were taken as essential to its fuller structural characterization; (b) the presentation, still at the first-level of evidence, of a purportedly exhaustive enumeration of the structural components of the practical arena, together with some indication of how they are disclosed as fitting together; and (c) the specification, now at the second-level of evidence, of a single and cohesive general structure which is exemplified and to some extent confirmed by the evidence at (a) and (b).

Now, the strain shows up differently in each of these phases. At (a), faithfulness to the practical arena as pretheoretically disclosed was paramount and, I would maintain, unexceptionable, but the achievement of theoretic availability was at a minimum. At (b), complete faithfulness was more questionable, both in regard to the details of structural components disclosed and the claim of comprehensiveness, but some higher degree of availability was gained. At (c), the demands of availability were more closely approached, but the very generality and structural preciseness of the proposal served to pull it still farther away from the insistency of the disclosures it was intended to cover. Still, I want to maintain, some additional increment of directive control upon ontological inquiry was gained at each of these successive phases. And with each of these gains some higher degree of viability of the ontological enterprise was, in effect, made apparent.

What is gained at (a) is this. The ontologist is constrained by such evidence to attend to it as indicating considerations which must be accommodated in his hypotheses. As such, they serve very much like alerts (as discussed in chapter 3), though with a basis of ontologically significant favor which most proposals along that line lack. Though this aid to ontological inquiry is genuine enough, it is not of a very high order. There are several reasons for this. First of all, since there are no conventions at the practical and pretheoretic level to which one can appeal for recording them, any manner of doing so will be largely evocative, i.e., such as to evoke a purportedly appropriate view of them. Second, even were their selection to be made on the basis of their intuitively obvious centricity in the practical arena, the fact that they are selections determines them to be fragmentary, unfinished, and thus conceivably misleading in a way which their being filled out in context would serve to mitigate. Third, their *prima facie* weight as relevant considerations cannot be taken at face value, for their larger contextual placement might well serve to diminish them or to bring other and weightier considerations to the fore. And fourth, the mere fact that they may be taken by the ontologist to deserve to be accounted for in some manner by his hypotheses or to be represented somehow in a system provides no clue at all as to how they might be so accommodated. It follows, then, that the effective control which such first-level considerations may provide for the ontologist's constructive efforts can never be more than minimal. Thus, the degree of viability which they can ensure can only be taken to be minimal as well.

It is easy to see that some of these limitations upon the serviceability of such pieces of evidence are mitigated by that expansion upon our understanding of them which comes with seeing them in the context of an overview of the terrain from which they are drawn. Phase (b) of my presentation proposed such a comprehending sketch. If it were found acceptable, the gain in evidential control upon ontological inquiry would be significant. In such a larger context a certain terminological solidification, though still pretheoretically based and largely evocative in function, can be encouraged. Appeal to a larger context of application is, I think, always an aid to the communication of reference. In addition, upon specification of an evidential consideration in its relevant comprehensive context, its apparently resultant evidential weight *vis-à-vis* other items in that context, though still intuitively set, is no longer unstable. Finally, the very unfinished and fragmentary character of isolated considerations is filled out, at least to some extent, by its placement in the larger and contextual view. In sum, what is proposed at (b) is a range of first-level evidence which is more carefully specifiable in its character, weight, and fullness than that which was or could be provided at (a). And this allows such evidence to be more available for ontological use and thus to ensure a still higher degree of viability for the enterprise.

There is also, of course, a gain along the road to the provision of a single and unified structure. What is offered is, though only nascently a structure, surely structural in a significant sense. But its shortcoming in this respect indicates as well an important limit to its serviceability. Indeed, it offers little advantage over the more scattered considerations at (a) in indicating how the ontologist is to account for it or represent it adequately in a hypothesis. After all, the ontologist has more to cover with his theory than the practical, and there are numerous ways, as the historical sweep of metaphysical speculation vividly illustrates, for attempting to save all of the appearances by relegating some of them to "mere appearance" or some other diminished status. Thus, nothing in the sketch provided at (b) can rule out, for example, a manner of accounting for the changing/enduring feature of the practical arena either by the elevation of change to a primary status and the denigration of endurance to a secondary and derivative one or vice versa. The fact that we are to favor the practical in all of its structural components cannot bar this, for each component will have been dealt with by theory and, indeed, treated as something which must be accounted for. Moreover, the primacy of the practical will have been honored to a significant degree by the proposal of such a theory; it will be honored precisely by providing an ultimately foundational role for a bedrock and structural component of the practical. We must not forget that there are always present to the ontologist those other and limiting controls on system-building which were discussed in chapter 2. And it is clear that an inquirer who rests content with the sort of minimally directive evidence which falls short of a cue, as that provided at (b) certainly is, will have to rely even more heavily on an appeal to the A-conditions of coherence, interpretive range, and informative impact. The point is that each of the ways of handling change and endurance which were indicated above may be proposed as satisfying these conditions. Of course, the adoption of the principle of avoiding any adjustment of the components which favors any sort of evidence which is drawn from some apractical manner of stancing may be taken as already justified. It cannot be denied that the ontologist's awareness of this is indeed something important and compelling. But, again, it provides no clear clue to how one is to go about constructing a theory which respects it. It provides, that is, no cue.

What is missing, it would seem, is a more rigorous reading of the structural components of the practical arena than is offered at (b), a reading which specifies their relative status in such a way that no adjustment to that status could be made without effectively replacing those components with other and different ones. Carrying such a structure forward into the process of construction would disallow the sort of overly selective appeal to the practical which was found to be allowable at the prior level. To serve this purpose, a structure need only be faithful to the first-level evidence in a very abstract way, so long, that is, as its invocation in inquiry can be supplemented by appeal to that evidence in an exemplifying role. If it were not so supplementable, then it would be incapable of serving this purpose, for the components which, by being bound together into a single package, are presumably to be forced equally upon our attention would become actually unavailable for our proper consideration. Thus, in order to provide the sort of global control at issue, both evidence of the sort proposed at (b) and a structure of the sort proposed at (c) must be carried forward in tandem. Insofar, then, as what is actually proposed at (c) provides adequately for one side of this role, it will represent a further gain in inquiry-directive control and, consequently, an additional increment in the elevation of viability.

But as significant for the furtherance of inquiry this coupling would prove to be, the structure proposed will not yet have achieved the office of a cue, of being available for fit, unless certain further conditions on it are fulfilled. I will now consider these conditions, the extent to which they might be fulfilled, and the difficulties which stand in the way of their ever being fulfilled completely.

4. Broadly speaking, there are two general conditions on a structure which is to serve as a cue in ontological inquiry, namely, faithfulness to the range of generic elements which are disclosed from favored access to

reality and serviceability for theoretic purposes. These conditions, as I have said, tend to pull in different directions, so that a perfect fulfillment of both by a single, fixed structure would appear to be impossible. One move which might be made in response to this is to propose that, nonetheless, a formulation of a structure may be accepted as a cue to the extent that it can be taken to include a sort of elasticity, to represent in effect a potentiality for at least a modest degree of interpretive stretch in each direction. Such a dynamic conception of a cue is in fact quite fitting to at least one previously discussed (at the end of section 8 in chapter 4) methodological service it may be expected to perform, namely, the service of admitting of some alterations towards the achievement of expansion to comprehensive scope without undermining its loyalty to the integrity of the practical arena. The fact remains that the stretch allowed cannot be too great, lest the dynamic tension fail and the extremes become so tenuously connected as to become strangers to each other. And the question is whether enough stretch towards theory to provide something which is significantly serviceable for fit can be tolerated.

Let us reconsider the proposal at (c) in this dynamic way, i.e., not as an attempt at a formally finished articulation of a disclosed structure, but as an attempt at an elastic model which can be stretched towards both pretheoretic and theoretic enhancement. Even considered as such, the limit of its stretch towards theory is obvious. This came out most strikingly no doubt in my somewhat agonized attempt to frame an ordering notion of "structural primacy" which would mimic a theoretically acceptable notion without employment of the regimenting relations of transitivity and symmetry or the system-inducing device of the allocation of entities by some such principles as the BOP. As I indicated, while faithfulness to the disclosures of the practical arena as they are found there precludes the application of theoretic devices which are not found there, the structure proposed was not intended to preclude one's eventually coming to understand the notion of structural primacy in more theoretically acceptable and systemically orderly terms. The point to be made here, however, is that the structure which was proposed could not, of itself, be stretched so far as to provide that understanding. And the further point ought to be made that it seems highly unlikely that any proposed cuing structure ever could. Still, I would say, something would be gained in the control of ontological construction with the sort of elastic but theoretically limited model which I proposed. That my attempt at (c) to formulate such a model was successful may well be doubted, but I would like to think that I succeeded in illustrating the sort of thing at issue. If I did that much, I would at least have shown its possibility and, in consequence, advanced the cause of viability still another notch.

5. Our pursuit of viability for the ontological enterprise has been en-
couraging. But we have now, it seems, come to an impasse on the narrow road we have taken. We may attempt to broaden the road a bit, and I
think we should, but how we might do that is a further story which I can
only hint at in this book. I will offer that hint in a moment. For the present, let me indicate the two barriers to our proceeding farther along our
present path.

These barriers are set by the two conditions on the theoretic serviceability of a cue which were first identified and discussed towards the end
of chapter 4, namely, the exhibition in its formulation of a certain theoretically available level of precision and its expandability towards comprehensive scope. I have just indicated why the first of these conditions
will be unsatisfiable to any further degree than that illustrated at (c). But
the barrier to expandability seems even more clearly insurmountable
and, since I have not yet emphasized that fact, I will take this opportunity
to do so now.

The difficulty about expandability is this. If the practical arena of itself
provided us with a structure which could be applied to an encompassing
world, then its elements of being incorrigibly localizing, centered, and
horizoned would have to be considered as inessential to it. But this
would be to get things backwards; though the practical arena does *not*
offer comprehensive scope, it *does* offer, at a bedrock and irremovable
level, a local scope which is determined by the purposes or projects
which arise in agent-thing interaction. From these considerations it follows as well that any attempt to expand a proposed structure of the practical arena towards comprehensive scope would be to reject one of its
components and thus to transform the entire structure into something
which is so different as to no longer merit the judgment of faithfulness.

How disappointing should we take this to be? Well, for one thing, we
need not, as I have argued above, conclude that we must chuck the entire project of showing the viability of the ontological enterprise. Some
decent degree of viability has already been shown. And it has not been
my object in this book to go beyond this. I wanted to set out the structure of the ontological enterprise, both in respect to its defining poles of
ground and goal and in respect to the pattern of its process of moving
from the one to the other, and then to argue for its meaningfulness, its
legitimacy, and, to a significant degree, its viability. Having now, at this
very point, completed these tasks, my discussion might well end here.

But surely there is more to be attempted, and it would indeed be disappointing if these somewhat arbitrary limitations on my own project
were seen to be limitations on further analysis. And I have not argued
that any further analysis must be unrewarding. One might, of course, ob-

serve that ontological inquiry cannot in any case be taken as a smooth and continuous development towards system. It confronts gaps throughout its course—the pretheoretic/theoretic one being only the most daunting—over which bridges cannot be built with any confidence but which, in the final analysis, can only be traversed by leaps of intuitive trust. But it is uncharacteristic of philosophers to rest content with any such picture. If not bridges—and I must say that I think they would be shaky in any case—then we would like to have some reason for thinking that our leaps may be made more promising. I may be excused, then, for closing my discussion by making some very general suggestions along this line.

6. I would like to suggest that what we need in order to move farther along the road to system is to broaden it by attempting to provide favor for *a way of having a world* which, by virtue of its inclusion of a purported comprehensive scope and a broader context of linguistic usage, is better able to accommodate both expandability and theoretically available precision. I am reconciled to the conclusion that nothing will ever take us all the way to theory, but it seems to me that, if we could identify some such way of having a world, it would aid us significantly.

Now, I do not think that there is any dearth of ways of having a world which we might consider, but of course we could only accept as serviceable a way which could be accorded ontological favor. And there is, I think, only one basis for according such favor. Since our favored access is practical stancing, it seems clear that only some broader dimension of our living could serve which, in addition to assuming the presence of a world and of ourselves in it, incorporated within its view, centrally and faithfully, the practical arena in its integrity. Favor could be gained only by preserving favored access in this way. The task, then, is to search for and attempt to identify such a world-providing yet arena-preserving way of life in regard to which pretheoretic survey is possible and a general structure of the world order it assumes is elicitable.

Before suggesting what this favored way of having a world might be, I would like to indicate a little more clearly what I mean to indicate by the phrase 'way of having a world' and how it differs from what we have come to understand stancing to be. I cannot attempt to go into detail about this, but several decisive considerations may be noted.

For the first, it should be clear by now that no manner of stancing posits a terrain which is understood, within that stancing considered as such and in isolation from its taking place in the broader context of one's life, to comprise everything there is, to circumscribe the universe, or to be identical to the world as a whole. Reflective attention to the reality-claim of a stance is of no help for this either, for though reference to being real may be made out in it, no reference to "reality" in any sense that could be taken as comprehensive is involved at all. Stancing, then, is not a way of having a *world*.

On the other hand, having a world is not a competitor in our lives with the stances we may take or find ourselves within. It is not at all a manner of disclosure, nor of thinking, acting, or anything of the like. Nothing is given to it or appears to it. Indeed, insofar as having a world involves the presence of anything in our lives, it rests upon and presupposes stancing of some manner or other. The simple fact is that, in the course of our concrete affairs, in the alternation of manners of stancing and our adjustment to them, we seem to develop a certain confidence in how things go, in our own overall orientation to things. How we manage this wondrous thing is not my concern here of course. But what emerges is something *like* our assuming that which it is the business of the ontologist to question and, if possible, better. The world we come to have may, surely, be ill-drawn, makeshift, unexamined, eccentric, fragmentary in unforeseen respects. As ontologists, we seldom attempt to make it explicit. But perhaps we should, if only to avoid giving over to the prejudice towards the development of system which it might exert on us unawares.

By the phrase 'having a world' I wish to indicate something "lived," i.e., something which is not necessarily thought and may never be examined but which is, when present, ingrained in one's life as a background to one's thinking, acting, believing, stancing, etc. As such, it is to be distinguished from the mere having or availability of the *concept* of a world, as well as from the cognitive and comparatively bloodless affairs of having the *belief that* there is a world or having a certain *worldview*. Nor is having a world to be taken as a mere *believing in* or acceptance of the presence of some world or other, for to have it is to count on it in certain more or less determinate ways, to rely upon its presence as making a difference in regard to what can be taken as real, important, or trustworthy. That is, to have a world is to orient oneself one way rather than another and in respect to a certain assumed order of things, even though, as is in fact typical, the specifics of this "world order" may never be brought to reflection or focal awareness.

Once we see what it is to have a world, what strikes us almost immediately is that there are several generically distinctive *ways* of having a world which may be shared with others and, along with each of these, a distinctive world order which is presupposed. It is popular in some philosophical circles to maintain that, at bottom, there is one and only one world order which is in fact ever assumed by us, as is indicated, it is sometimes supposed, by our shared language, basic needs as human beings, or social projects. This seems to me supportable, if it is supportable at all, only at a level of formal analysis which is much more removed from our lives than what I have in mind. What I have in mind as a way of having a world is indeed something quite general and shareable, but it is also something which provides footing and orientation in day-to-day affairs and is consequently already interpreted, provided with application, to the wide variety of sorts of things we take account of in our experience. Thus, the deeply religious person assumes a different way of things than does the nonreligious and scientistic person, and the historicalist (I don't say the historicist, for that term is used to indicate a sort of theorist) and the aesthete assume different ways yet. The diversity of such ways is not so different from that which was proposed by Ernst Cassirer as indicating the diversity among what he preferred to call symbolic forms or manners of consciousness: ordinary language, myth, religion, history, science, and art. He went beyond the specification of these, however, to argue that each is grounded in a sort of Kantian substructure which represents, at a very deep level, the assumed order of any possible symbolic form. I doubt that we can go along with him so far, but, even if we could, it is not the assumption of such a deep structure which I am attempting to mark out as a way of having a world, but the diverse yet still general manners of consciousness which exemplify it.

Each such way of having a world is consuming. As providing one's widest and most reliable set of assumptions regarding how things are ordered, each exhibits a sort of inertia in regard to one's manner of living which is difficult to deflect or alter. Such difficulty is not impossibility, however, and something less than "conversion" may allow shift. In any event, in spite of the inertia of that way of having a world which is present at a certain point in one's life, one is not necessarily precluded from entertaining or imagining what would be involved in at least some other ways. In fact, I would want to argue that there is one such way which is pretty much available to each of us as representing our first and often submerged, but seldom entirely overcome, manner of finding ourselves in a world. And this is the one which I want to propose as our only reasonable candidate for a favored way of having a world.

In the final analysis, I think, the most appropriate name for this favored way is 'the mythic'. At first blush, however, this appellation seems outrageously unbefitting for something which is to serve us on the road to a system which is true of reality. Clearly, something must be said in behalf of my employment of it. I cannot do much about this here. I will be content to make the point that appeal to the mythic world order as a favored surrogate for the structure of the practical arena is hardly as appalling as it will surely look to one who takes the word 'myth' to carry the sense of 'falsehood' or 'mere fabrication' or to include some essential reference to such suspect things as magic and metamorphosis. The fact that in the mythic world, at least as it has been "primitively" or archaically lived, all sorts of magical and other wildly improbable events seem to be thought to occur only serves to indicate its structural generosity. None of these things are, it seems to me, built into the mythic world order as such; it is just that that order may be fleshed out in a number of ways, some of which may encourage acceptance of such things and some of which may not. But if such a world order would seem to some people to allow too much, it seems to me clear that every other candidate allows much too little. And the critical point is this: every other world order contrives either to destabilize or reorder the practical arena or to localize it or practical stancing itself in a role of unimportance relative to some concern or commitment which is taken to be supreme or overriding. And this is clearly ontologically spoiling. For, however deep and ineradicable such a concern or commitment might be and however significant the elevation of that concern may be taken to be for the purpose of providing a personal sense of meaning in one's life, it can have no status which would be such as to override the ontological favor to be accorded to the practical stance.

My suggestion is, then, that we consider the possibility that the mythic way of having a world provides a world order which can be articulated as a cue or at least as a nonspoiling stand-in for the cue which we could never quite provide on the narrow basis of consideration of the structure of the practical arena. It is, after all, the first in human history and the first in our lives, it remains to some extent present in each of our lives, it is to some extent elicitable from our lives (though I would suggest only with a great deal of help from considerations of an ethnological sort), and it is the only way of having a world which includes and preserves the integrity of the practical arena. How each of these claims may be supported is, as you might expect, a very long story, but it is, I think, a compelling story and one which can be told. I trust I will be excused for saving it for another volume.

Notes

1. The phrase 'something m appears as x being F' is intended to be quite noncommittal regarding the best analysis of "appearing as." The point of employing 'm' as well as 'x' as a reference is *not* to indicate a "thing" which is distinct from the "thing" indicated by 'x', but merely to provide a simplified way of referring to the appearance as a whole. And it does abbreviate some of our reports of how things appear, e.g., when we say, "There's a red pencil." Unfortunately, it may mislead one into a certain view of "appearing as" which seems to me quite mistaken, namely, that something m is that which in fact appears but is taken or judged to be something else n, e.g., that though what in fact appears to us are some marks on a blackboard, we immediately interpret them as or take them to be a figure of an animal (a duck, let us say) and thereby tend to misreport what appears to us as an animal figure. This confusion is addressed and disentangled in chapter 4.
2. This point is an ancient one and derives, so far as I can tell, from the later skeptical tradition. Sextus Empiricus summarizes the skeptical attitude towards appearances as an "acquiescence" to them without further judgment as to what they may be taken by others to be evidence of, e.g., the nonevident or "hidden" (36, 38). The notion of acquiescence is borrowed from everyday social transactions; it carries with it the notion of something presenting itself as, we might say, "requesting" acquiescence. And if appearances may be acquiesced to, then they must be taken as making a claim for our acceptance, which is not imposed on them externally or by proxy but is rather inextricably involved in them as they appear. They are not just indifferent data, but in their appearing to us they push themselves on us in such a way that, if we are outwardly passive to them, we involuntarily give over to them.
3. In *Man and People*, Ortega y Gasset makes the point very well, though he is actually attempting to characterize our lives as we live them from day to day rather than the practical stance as such.

> Things are not originally "things," but something that I try to use or avoid in order to live and to live as well as possible; are, therefore, that with which I occupy myself and by which I am occupied, with which I act and operate, with which I succeed or fail to do what I want to do; in short, they are concerns to which I am constantly attending. And since "to do" and "to occupy oneself," "to have concerns" is expressed in Greek by "practice," *praxis*—things are radically *pragmata* and my relation to them is *pragmatic*. . . . A thing as *pragma*, then, is something that I manipulate for a particular end, that I deal with or avoid, that I must count upon or discount; it is an instrument or an impediment *for*: a task, a chattel, a gadget, a deficiency, a failure, an obstacle; in short, it is a concern to be attended to, something that to a greater or less degree is of import for me, that I lack, that I have too much of, hence an *importance*. (MP 54–55)

Heidegger apparently held a similar view. Cf. *Being and Time*, 96–97. (I say "apparently" because I do not altogether understand him or what he is up to and shall surely be accused of misinterpretation by his devotees if I am not cagey.)

4. I employ the term 'cast' in order to avoid begging the issue by the use of such theoretically loaded terms as 'property' or 'quality'. The picture of a practical situation as consisting of (among other things) particulars, properties, and relations is not a picture which conforms to it as it appears in everyday practical affairs. Moreover, nothing specific is indicated in the formulation by the term 'things which are', which is simply to be taken as covering whatever constituents of reality there may be. Perhaps this formulation of the reality-claim is misleading to the extent that it suggest a very simple but still antecedently adopted theory to the effect that reality consists of at least two distinct items, namely, "things" and their characters. No such theory is intended. The point is simply that practical cast is in reality.

5. For this I have adapted to my own purposes the formulation of Annas and Barnes (25).

6. That's why, I suspect, he appended to his discussion of the fourth mode the more general argument against favoring S or S^* which is derived from the five modes of Agrippa.

7. The notion of *true-of* which is involved deserves further discussion than I will give it. Let me only say that I take it to be primitive and distinct from the "is true" which is attached to propositions, sentences, or beliefs. The point in the text is that such a claim is made, even though problems remain of what is to count as a system, what is to count as reality, and what is to count as being true of.

8. Thus we have another sort of reality-claim, though in this case about a system rather than about the appearance of things in a stance. But the move to identify as the same the reality referred to in both sorts of claim may be anticipated.

9. For a further discussion of this, though not always convincing, see Körner, especially 8–10.

10. One may also raise the issue of the very possibility of categoreal change, an issue which does not admit of decision by convention but which is also tangential to our task. In any case, I have discussed the matter at some length elsewhere ("On Changing One's Categories," *Metaphilosophy* 9, nos. 3 and 4 [July/October 1978]).

11. The Quinean analysis of ontic commitment, though seriously flawed, takes just this approach. I have attempted to show why it is flawed and how its "application" is spoiled by systemic regimentation in my article "Quine and the Ontological Enterprise," *Review of Metaphysics* 26, no. 3 (March 1973).

12. I will resist the almost overwhelming urge to illustrate by reference to my own work (in "The Subject-Matter of Metaphysics," *Southwestern Journal of Philosophy* 2, nos. 1 and 2 (Spring and Summer, 1971), and "Quine and the Ontological Enterprise") how I think this analysis is to be carried forward in detail and what its results would be.

13. For example, in *Act and Agent*, chapter 2.

14. If Dewey is taken to have the practical arena in mind after all, which I doubt, we may be inclined to excuse him, grudgingly, as merely being inattentive or perhaps speaking loosely. Much the same may be said for Ortega y Gasset, who seems typically to employ the term 'world' as a synonym for 'circumstance', a poor substitution for sure. We cannot, however, say as much for someone like Heidegger, for whom this confusion appears to represent (though I may be wrong about this, given my own difficulty in understanding him) a fundamental philosophical lapse.

15. Clarification of the "relation" of "having structural primacy over" by appeal to standard logical relations is difficult to avoid. The merit which attaches to the avoidance

of appeal to any systemic ordering, namely, that it *might* be distorting and ultimately question-begging in some unforeseen fashion, would seem to be balanced by the promise of being able by such means to better grasp the "relation" in question. For example, it seems appropriate and illuminating to characterize "structural primacy over," "grounded in," and "depends on" as transitive, the first as asymmetrical, and the last two as nonsymmetrical. The urge to reformulate the given expansion on "structural primacy over" in terms of the sufficient and necessary conditions exemplified by an implication between propositions is less immediately illuminating.

16. Whether this primacy of individual over arena can be adequately accounted for in terms of reduction, emergence, supervenience, or some other ontological relation is, of course, a topic of theoretic interest and therefore not germane to the present pretheoretic task. An appeal to any such devices of account and explanation, even in behalf of achieving clarity, would be spoiling at this level of investigation, though I think it is clear that an appeal to intrasystemic reductionistic or, correlatively, constructionistic devices at *any* level would be confusing and inappropriate. Intersystemic reduction is, however mysterious, another matter entirely.

Bibliography

Only editions cited or referred to in the text are listed. Dates of original publication, if different from these editions, are indicated in parentheses. Abbreviations used in references in the text, if any, are indicated after date of publication.

Annas, Julia, and Barnes, Jonathan. *The Modes of Skepticism*. New York: Cambridge University Press, 1985.

Browning, Douglas. *Act and Agent*. Miami, FL: University of Miami Press, 1964.

—— "On Changing One's Categories." *Metaphilosophy* 9, nos. 3 and 4 (July/October 1978): 212–25.

—— "Quine and the Ontological Enterprise." *Review of Metaphysics* 26, no. 3 (March 1973): 492–510.

—— "The Subject-Matter of Metaphysics." *Southwestern Journal of Philosophy* 2, nos. 1 and 2 (Spring and Summer 1971): 103–15.

Christian, William A. "Some Uses of Reason." In *The Relevance of Whitehead*, edited by Ivor Leclerc. London: Allen and Unwin, 1961.

Dewey, John. *Experience and Nature*. 2d ed.; New York: W. W. Norton, 1929. References are to *John Dewey: The Later Works, 1925–1953*, vol. 1. Edited by Jo Ann Boydston. Carbondale: Southern Illinois University Press, 1981.

—— *Logic: The Theory of Inquiry* (1938). References are to *John Dewey: The Later Works, 1925–1953*, vol. 12. Edited by Jo Ann Boydston. Carbondale: Southern Illinois University Press, 1986.

—— "The Need for a Recovery in Philosophy" (1917). References are to *John Dewey: The Middle Works, 1899–1924*, vol. 10. Edited by Jo Ann Boydston. Carbondale: Southern Illinois University Press, 1980.

—— "Does Reality Possess Practical Character?" (1908). In *John Dewey: The Middle Works, 1899–1924*, vol. 4. Edited by Jo Ann Boydston. Carbondale: Southern Illinois University Press, 1977.

Hall, Everett W. *Philosophical Systems, A Categorial Analysis*. Chicago: University of Chicago Press, 1960.

Harman, Gilbert. *The Nature of Morality*. New York: Oxford University Press, 1977.

Heidegger, Martin. *Being and Time* (1927). Translated by John Macquarrie and Edward Robinson. 1927; New York: Harper and Row, 1962.

James, William. *The Principles of Psychology* (1890). Cambridge, MA: Harvard University Press, 1981 and 1983.

Körner, Stephan. *Categorial Frameworks*. London: Basil Blackwell, 1970.

Mackie, J. L. *Ethics: Inventing Right and Wrong*. New York: Penguin Books, 1977.

Ortega y Gasset. José. *Man and People*. Translated by Willard R. Trask. New York: W. W. Norton, 1957. (*MP*)

———— *Meditations on Quixote* (1914). Translated by Evelyn Rugg and Diego Marin. New York: W. W. Norton, 1961. (*MQ*)

———— *Some Lessons in Metaphysics.* Translated by Mildred Adams. 1966; New York: W. W. Norton, 1969. The original lectures were delivered in 1932–33. (*SLM*)

Pepper, Stephen C. *World Hypotheses, A Study in Evidence.* Berkeley: University of California Press, 1942.

Sextus Empiricus. *Sextus Empiricus: Selections from the Major Writings on Scepticism, Man, & God.* Edited by Philip P. Hallie. Rev. ed. Cambridge: Avatar Books; Indianapolis: Hackett Publishing, 1985.

Strawson, P. F. *Skepticism and Naturalism: Some Varieties.* New York: Columbia University Press, 1985.

Whitehead, Alfred North. *Modes of Thought.* New York: Cambridge University Press, 1938. (*MT*).

———— *Process and Reality* (1929). Corrected ed. Edited by David Ray Griffin and Donald W. Sherburne. New York: Free Press, Macmillan, 1978. Cited pagination is of 1929 Macmillan edition. (*PR*)

Index

Terms are indexed only for definitive or otherwise significant passages.
All proper names are indexed.

Reality-claim question, 26–30, 33–34
Reflection, 4, 13, 19–20, 23–26, 28–29, 33–34, 57
Risk, 136
Russell, Bertrand, xii

S-conditions, 39–41, 74
Seeing as, 91, 93
Sense-providing home, 17
Sextus Empiricus, 32–33, 159
Sorts, 128, 137
    See also Natural sorts
Space, 126–27, 142
Speculation, 5, 70, 73–74
Speculative controls, 74, 76; directive, 75, 151, limiting, 74–75
Stance, Stancing, 5, 11–24, 27, 35, 58–59, 84, 117, 129–31, 154–55; apractical, 21–22, 116; moral, 29–32; practical, 5–6, 20–22, 30–31, 35, 109, 118, 121, 125, 127, 130, 134, 146, 154, 157, 160; practical, primacy of, 113–18, 130; theoretical, 114, 126, 131
Stancer, 15, 17, 23
    See also Agent, stancing
Standpoint, 9–12, 20; "detached," 10–12, 14–16, 19–20; "involved," 5, 10–11, 14–16, 19–20

Strawson, P. F., xi, 5, 9–16, 19–20, 25–29
Structural primacy, 137–40, 152, 160–61
Structure, 55, 58, 78–82, 85, 98–110, 137, 142, 151–52; functional, 106
Subject, 23, 126
Survey, 5, 62, 65–69, 73, 84, 123–25, 154
System, 2–4, 24, 38–41, 58
    See also Ontology, system of
Systemic claims, 45

Terms: cartographical, 64, 88, 94; technical, 87–88
Terrain, 17, 127, 132, 154
Theory, 45, 55, 137
Things, 12, 23, 126–28, 133–34
Time, 126–27, 142
Transystemic claims, 42, 45
'True of', 37, 64, 160

Understanding, 39–40
Universal science, 2–3, 5, 38–39, 52, 54, 66, 68–69, 81, 84

Whitehead, A. N., xi, xii, 39, 41–42, 44, 49–50, 52–54, 66, 75–83
Wittgenstein, Ludwig, xi
World, 153–55, 157, 160; having a, 155; in the, 132, 156; way of having a, 6, 154–57